Behind the Baton

BEHIND THE BATON

Charles Blackman

1964 | CHAROS ENTERPRISES, INC. | NEW YORK

Carl Fischer, Inc.   Sole Selling Agents
56–62 Cooper Square, New York 3, N. Y.
Boston—Chicago—Dallas

Dedicated to my wife
with love and gratitude for her unending faith.

My deepest appreciation and heartfelt thanks to all the people who have, by the statements they so generously contributed, immeasurably enhanced this book.

I also wish to acknowledge a debt of gratitude to my friends and colleagues who read the manuscript in various stages, criticized and encouraged me.

Charles Blackman

Contents

Preface

This book arises out of two factors—a long, practical experience and intimate association with orchestras and conductors, as well as the conviction that there is a growing misconception of their relative functions and responsibilities.

It would seem, at first glance, that there need be no difficulty in grasping the role of the modern conductor. After all, he works in a blazing glow of publicity, and it appears to many that what he is doing on the podium is, or should be, fairly obvious. And there is no lack of texts on the "How to" of the conductor's art in which his function is neatly prescribed in elaborate rule of procedure, guides to gesture, and so forth.

Yet the matter, on any kind of serious analysis, especially from "inside the profession" so to speak, turns out not to be that simple, and the further one delves into the subject the more does diversity of opinion and the widest variations of practice begin to appear.

The conductor as we know him today is, one must recognize, only a recent development in the history of music, and even within the past three or four generations there have been conspicuous differences in his procedures, in his relation to his players, and the way in which the musical public views his role.

From the days when the composer was his own conductor down to the day of the virtuoso conductor (or glamorized public idol), the changes have been notable indeed. With such changes, and with diverse methods of educating conductors and choosing them, many distortions and obscurities have developed. At the same time great conductors have made their appearance, men and musicians of a type not known or needed before.

In this metamorphosis, a certain air of mystery has arisen as to just how the creative musical and social function of the conductor (for he is a voice of the community whose music he helps to make) is carried out, or, how it can be warped or evaded even by men who are not obscure in the field.

My personal interest prompted me to make an extensive survey of opinions held by people involved with orchestral performance in various sections of the country. I spoke with conductors, music educators, instrumentalists and Board members. The information I acquired justified my belief that there is confusion on the essential points of the subject, and there is something wrong in the philosophy of the training of conductors. If this is true within the profession, a corresponding confusion among the public is not surprising.

Undoubtedly, one or another phase of this complex art may be readily understood. The reader may find ideas here which will seem to him to need little elaboration; but he will also find here what I am convinced is widely lacking, and that is, a fully worked out exposition of the total function and interrelation of the modern conductor, score, orchestra and audience.

My purpose is to present a comprehensive view of the conductor's role, and portray the entity called "conductor" in dimensions which will enable the reader to appreciate the importance of the "WHY" of his craft as well as the "HOW." Toward the realization of this end, I am privileged to be able to present the opinions of many distinguished, dedicated authorities who are vital participants in the contemporary musical world. The insights contained in their statements, so generously provided, will help to bring into sharp focus the entity "Behind the Baton."

C. B.

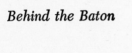

Behind the Baton

1 | *The conductor*

What is he?

The cynosure of all eyes, he appears in a different light to the audience, his players, the composers, and each group endows him with certain characteristics according to their point of view and areas of reference. These imputed characteristics range from almost super-human powers, with special gifts and faculties, to mere mechanical proficiency.

I should like to strip the entity called "Conductor" clear of any aura of mystery, examine its physical structure, its function and motivation, and cut out and lay bare its sinews and muscles for detailed inspection.

Everyone who takes part in an orchestral performance —including the audience—should be familiar with the hidden elements of this entity. The conductor, in particular, must be able to look at his own dissected image and understand the minutest details of the forces available to him, before he can intelligently dedicate himself to the enormous task and responsibility to which he aspires.

To begin with, it is pertinent to ask, "How did the conductor come into existence?" The conductor, as we know him, is a comparatively new factor in the performance of ensemble music. But was he invented? Did someone, at a given point in history, decide that the audiences would listen more attentively if they were given a central figure to concentrate on? Was it because the musicians suddenly became incapable of playing without the help of a composer or his emissary who could explain, by gestures, that which had already been written? Or was it because orchestral writing developed to a stage so complex that the players were too far removed from each other in the harmonic structure and musical form to be able to absorb all the other parts and coordinate themselves without help? Every serious music student should know the answers to these questions. Yet, it is surprising to see how many minify the fact that the conductor, and his function, was necessitated by the needs of composers and players. And all too few, both in the audience and in the musical community, are fully aware of the complexities of his art.

Thus there is a noticeable, indeed disturbing tendency to confuse the "act" of conducting with the "art" of conducting. The impression that a conductor's movements seem to coincide with the musical utterances of an orchestra does not prove that he is actually conducting it, in the true sense of the word. His motions might be as well coordinated with a recording producing the music. The delicate difference between conducting an orchestra and conducting while an orchestra plays is in the application of "purpose and reason." This could also be said to be the difference between the "art" of conducting and the "act" of conducting.

To practice his art, the conductor must approach his orchestra for and with a musical purpose, and have a reason for every move he makes; a reason based on his knowledge of the composer's wishes, and a concept of the involuntary reaction the move will call forth. In this respect, he can be compared with a fine painter who knows, in advance, what will result from the use of certain colors in placement on the canvas, in mixture, in dilution, in reflection, even in subsequent deterioration.

In the search for reason, we are confronted with two widely accepted but opposing theories regarding the purpose and function of the contemporary conductor. One school of thought, supported by many conductors, contends that conducting, or the ability to conduct, is instinctive; and believes that if the student will learn to read his score and understand the character of the music, he will, somehow, find a way to make his intentions

known to the orchestra. The importance of specific physical discipline being thereby minimized. This idea is advanced in all sincerity with a view toward preserving
the individuality of the conductor.

The opposite theory asserts that conducting is primarily a form of communication, and, as with any language, there must be recognizable signs and symbols;
in this instance, physical motions. The proponents of this
approach maintain the belief that a conductor with a
larger physical vocabulary has a correspondingly wider
scope for individual expression.

Both theories are well-intentioned. But, in practice,
will they obtain equal results under similar conditions,
or good results under varying conditions? The carefully
selected personnel of major orchestras brings to the performance as much knowledge and ability as does the
conductor. Generally within this favored group, it is not
technical clarification but musical individuality which
sets one conductor's concept apart from another. It is
easy, then, for some conductors who have good orchestras to feel that their technical proficiency, in itself, is
not of primary importance. And because their position,
as Musical Directors of first-rate symphonies, carries an
implication of superior knowledge, their views are often
accepted as unquestionable fact by many who may be
unaware of the hidden errors and distortions in this easy
but unjustified assumption.

The fact is, a conductor is not always privileged to
direct a group of highly trained and routined instru-

mentalists. More often, he will be faced with players who need his help in every detail of performance, including the fundamental technique of their own instruments. In such a situation, the conductor subscribing to the first theory is at a serious disadvantage. Besides his inability to give technical guidance, he places an additional burden upon the players in the nature of his individual method of communication. Out of obvious necessity, therefore, after several painful encounters with different orchestras, this conductor must eventually, at least to some extent, utilize the essentials of a standard technical method. Perhaps the improvement resulting from such change in method lends credence to yet another opinion that conducting can be learned only through trial and error. However, there is no qualified evidence to prove that this is either true or practical. By the time a conductor is afforded even limited opportunity for experimentation, it is often too late to develop the fine physical dexterity and smooth coordination necessary.

Then, of course, there are the so-called human or psychological factors with which conductors in both camps must concern themselves. On the one hand, there is the individual human being that is each member of his orchestra, and on the other, the variables his listeners will bring to bear—their composite mood, intent, intellectual preparation—all of which influence their musical impression. For the conductor it is even more important, than for the painter, to fully understand the values of these factors. Unlike a painting, the re-creation of music is always immediate and irrevocable. And, since the conductor's medium is made up of skilled human beings—in place of brushes, tubes of paint and canvas—mistakes in judgment and execution cannot be changed or erased. All of the myriad number of elements involved in the production of each sound must be weighed in the conductor's mind, and the proper gesture chosen with the conviction that the reactions of the players will be the ones desired.

This process of action and reaction is a most interesting one. The performance of an orchestral composition requires a continuous, coordinated series of actions by the conductor for the purpose of stimulating reactions from the orchestra. These reactions, in turn, seek to evoke the ultimate emotional response of the listener. In effect, the orchestra is somewhat like a mirror, and might be said to fulfill a similar function, subject to one reservation. Whereas a mirror always reflects truthfully anything that is placed before it, whether it is clear or vague, an orchestra faced with a vague subject can, if it wishes, clarify the image through its own knowledge of the subject before it. It is far from uncommon that an orchestra will produce a clearer musical reflection than the conducting image before it.

The exercise of this option by orchestras has prompted many conductors to claim the clarified image as their own. It has also lulled many into a dependency upon such clarification or correction, and has allowed them to take unearned credit and praise. Both of these errors in judgment stem from the same source—a fundamental insecurity.

There are many reasons for this insecurity. However, most of them can be eliminated if the conductor understands and accepts his true function, authority and responsibility. Confidence is further enhanced by a thorough physical preparation which develops the necessary muscular strength and conditioned reflexes needed to carry out his function. And, equally important, an appreciation of how much the orchestra is prepared to contribute should remove any remaining uncertainty.

In order to acquire this insight into the orchestra's role, one must have more than a casual acquaintanceship with the orchestral instruments themselves; the various methods of playing, orthodox and otherwise; the extremes possible for each instrument; and the mental attitudes skilled and unskilled players maintain toward their conductor. Ideally, every potential conductor should be technically proficient on several orchestral instruments, and spend a number of years playing at least one instrument of each orchestral section in different symphonic organizations, under as many conductors as possible. But by whatever method achieved, only a complete mastery of all the elements of his art can endow the conductor with the self-confidence which will leave him completely free to concentrate on the musical thought; secure in the knowledge that the execution will follow the intent as surely and smoothly as his mind absorbs the score.

It has been widely argued that many of our most highly respected conductors had no specific or formal study of their craft. Their worth was discovered when, through some unfortunate circumstance, a scheduled conductor could not appear, and an atmosphere was created in which a genius could rise from the ranks as if by magic, equipped with unlimited knowledge, extensive preparation and superb control. Magic, miracles and hero worship are ever present in the minds of men, though sometimes smothered beneath rationalized sophistication. It is no surprise, therefore, that few really wish to seek out and analyze the psychological factors which come into play at so dramatic a moment. The heightened tension, the instant and complete concentration of the orchestra, and the subconscious resolve by every player to avoid any possible mishap coupled with their collective knowledge and experience, combine to create a sharp, accurate and stimulating performance not due entirely to the ability, however fine, of the newly discovered conductor.

It is indisputable that many of those favored by such opportunities had worked hard and long preparing themselves for any eventuality which might afford them an opportunity to display their accomplishments. They have gone on to prove their right to the praise heaped upon them. Others have lived out their lives (some with great fame) without realizing that the music made by

their orchestras was made in spite of them, not because
of them. The publicity usually attendant upon the "Cin-
derella" instances has helped to raise doubts in the mind
of the aspirant for a conductor's post. He sometimes
finds it difficult to decide whether to devote himself to
"study and prayer," as it were, or concentrate upon trying to be in the right place at the right time.

| .... |

Another error common in theorizing about conducting,
whether by professional or layman, arises from the in-
discriminate use of easy words and phrases to describe
the act of conducting. They are confused by contradic-
tory terminology. Conducting has been called an art, a
craft, an instinct and even an instinctive art. It is one
thing for the layman to accept a convenient label or
description, but it is most important for the conductor
to know what these words really mean, and how they
apply to him.

Let us examine accepted dictionary definitions of
some of these words. To begin with, "Conductor" means
*"a leader; a guide; one who goes before or accompanies;
one who shows the way."* Also, it means *"a supervisor; a
manager; and, in fact, a contractor who brings various
elements together."* This would seem to indicate that
there is a large element of aid and instruction involved,
rather than power and command.

The words "art" and "instinct"—so often misused—
have an interesting juxtaposition. The dictionary tells us

art is *"the disposition or modification of things by human skills to answer the purpose intended."* Additionally, it is *"a system of rules serving to facilitate the performance of certain actions, acquired by experience, study or observation."* In other words, art is an intellectually guided physical skill applied to the accomplishment of a rational purpose. Instinct, on the other hand, is defined as *"impulse, power or disposition which is independent of instruction, without deliberation, and without having any previously reasoned end in view."* In a broader sense, it is a *"natural qualification for some specialty,"* but a propensity which can manifest itself only through the training, study and resultant skills in the practice of any art.

This is not to imply that the words "art" and "instinct" have no direct relationship. *The danger lies in substituting the meaning of one for the demands of the other.* The "art" of conducting demands the keenest mental discipline plus highly developed craftsmanship and great physical stamina. The "instinct" for conducting is that "sixth sense" which stimulates and guides the application of the acquired "art." Mastery of the "art" can make a fine conductor, but the addition of his "instinct" can make him great. Conversely, the strongest instinct without the craftsmanship necessary to the art will result in correspondingly deep frustration.

With the clarification of these terms we are prepared to examine the function, authority and responsibility of the modern conductor.

2 | *Function*

The primary function of a conductor is communication. Through various physical actions, he is required to indicate to the players all of the instructions contained in the score, plus all that may be implied by the score, or understood as a result of diligent study and research. This conception will surely appear unexceptionable to the reader or any student of the subject.

Actually, the orchestra members have music in front of them containing instructions. They can read them, they can perform their parts individually, they can hold meetings and agree to play their several parts at a single tempo, a single mood, and, through discussion, arrive at what could be considered a knowledgeable rendition of the composer's intent. Why, then, should a conductor be necessary?

One reason is purely physical. Though each player may have the same intent, as previously agreed upon, it is almost impossible in a modern orchestra for each player to hear every other one in the orchestra, and, at the same time, anticipate problems that might arise from instrumental and technical mishaps, take into account the acoustical problems of the auditorium at the time of performance, and adjust his rate of breathing to that of one hundred other people. Breath control is one of the particularly important though hidden requirements for good ensemble performance, for without the unified breath control there cannot be a unified phrase control.

Therefore, the conductor must be prepared to indicate to his players, all of whom are already occupied with the technical aspects of their instruments, all of those factors which the players cannot indicate to each other at the time of performance. He must, mainly by the motions of his hands, make clear the exact tempo and the phrasing as it should be enunciated by the various instruments, indicate in advance and control the dynamic level of each choir, try to anticipate any possible technical difficulties that might confront any player, and coordinate the rate of breathing so important for a coherent musical expression. All this must be done simultaneously and continuously throughout the composition if the conductor is to exercise creatively the

full range of his function. Any relaxation of control, however slight, in the physical functions of conducting
constitutes a surrender of leadership, for during such
periods of no control the players are forced to assume
the musical responsibility themselves, and the result is,
at the very least, an uneven performance.

Some conductors mistakenly dismiss the need for
continuous control by saying that the players are competent enough to be left alone for periods of time when
the conductor wishes to concern himself solely with the
line of the composition. This may be true to a certain
extent; but we must remember that each player looks up
at the conductor at a different moment, according to the
demands of the music, and it is the function of the conductor to see that the directions he gives are available
to each player whenever he may look for them. The
assurance that he can check his place in the complex
structure of a symphonic composition at any time encourages the player to follow without question or concern.

The physical skill necessary to maintain this control
consistently and clearly is commonly referred to as "the
technique of the conductor." This is the facet of the conductor's art which is most obvious to orchestra and audience and, consequently, strongly affects the ultimate
reactions of both. There are, of course, those who contend this physical technique is not necessary, that it is
old-fashioned, and that it inhibits the conductor in his
"interpretations." While this opinion may be offered by

those who feel the lack of such physical dexterity, there is no logical reason why a conductor's technique should detract from his musical freedom any more than the facile technique of an instrumentalist detracts from his musical expression. On the contrary, the more technique available in any area of performance, the more freedom of expression the performer can allow himself. Only a clumsy or inefficient physical technique can impede a conductor, just as it would a player.

We know from past experience and very seriously prepared experiments, that an orchestra without a conductor has a more difficult time achieving the qualities its members would like in their performance than one with a properly trained conductor. But if the conductor is not to exercise the true functions of his position; that is, if the conductor is not to do, by means of his technique, that which the players cannot do for themselves, then, again, we are faced with the question, why the conductor?

Therefore, no conductor may arbitrarily decide that any of the elements of his total responsibility do not apply to him, nor can he successfully substitute one of the necessary elements for another. They are fundamentals that govern intelligent leadership in any situation. A conductor must lead, and a leader must be capable of deciding where his group should go, how they are to get there, and translate his directions so they can be easily followed. The very nature of music, with its wide variety and constant change, makes it imperative that the directions be issued in such manner that they are quickly understood, yet with a minimum of distraction. The value of a conductor's knowledge lies only in his ability to effectively transmit that knowledge to the orchestra.

We have reached the stage in our social behavior during orchestral performance where only one method of communication is considered acceptable. That method is visual. Since we have outgrown the music director who pounded a stick on the floor to keep time for the orchestra—and I am sure we would be equally disconcerted if, in our concert halls, we were to hear the conductor shouting instructions to the players in the loud passages or whispering them through the soft ones—we have no choice but to substitute visual signals. The choice is completely justified. As the spoken word is disciplined and used to form recognizable patterns, so can the visual motions (technique) be disciplined and standardized for all to understand.

But an ability to communicate visually is only a part of the conductor's responsibility to and for the orchestra. He is expected to be all things to all the players at once; convincing authority, teacher, champion, guide, and in effect, the orchestra's musical conscience. This is, indeed, a great challenge.

In order to properly evaluate this composite role, it is necessary to understand exactly what "an orchestra's musical conscience" means. Does it mean that the conductor must try to perform a given composition according to the varying knowledge and emotional concept of each player, striving to arrive at a common exposition that would satisfy everyone a little bit? Or is he to assume that his position gives him the right to follow the dictates of his own musical conscience and impose this upon the orchestra? It can be argued that, by virtue of his rank, he directs and controls the musical thought, correspondingly bears the brunt of criticism and praise, and, therefore, his musical conception should be accepted, without question, precisely as he indicates it.

The fallacy of this too facile logic lies in the fact that the conductor is not subject to the conscience of the players, nor solely to his own personal conscience. His function is to weld together a force, of which he is a most vital part, in subservience to the *intent* and *conscience* of the composer. It is not his privilege to function as critic or censor of the composer's intentions. On the contrary, by accepting the very authority which empowers him to choose the compositions, he is obliged to assume the composer's thoughts as his own and instill them into the consciousness of the orchestra. This makes his task a formidable one. One which calls for much more than a familiarity with the notes in a score and a set of stereotyped gestures. Many diverse requirements, both physical and mental must be met without qualification, coupled with an integrity that will not allow him to rationalize any compromise he may be tempted to make in the absence of one or more of these important requirements.

In the execution of all of his duties, the conductor has the cooperation of a sensitive instrument (the orchestra) willing and anxious to respond to his directions. The results he obtains vary in proportion to his technical facility, and the assurance with which he uses it to honestly re-create the intentions of the composer. A capable conductor, fully aware of all this, can never shift to the orchestra any defect or failure of his own.

There is still another function which the conductor must consider carefully. Since, in the performance, he is the focal point of attention, it is incumbent upon him to so direct this attention that the listeners become completely absorbed with the musical sound, while being helped to follow the line and content of the composition —much like an instructor tracing a route on a map with a pointer as he describes the course to be followed. As long as there is physical movement involved, the sight as well as the hearing of the audience should be coordinated with the sights and sounds emanating from the stage. If the conductor can, through his movements, stimulate the physical response of the audience to the extent that they breathe collectively with the phrase and rhythmic pattern of the music, he will have achieved the ultimate in communication between the composer and the audience.

However, his relationship with the audience does not, under any circumstances, condone pretentious or flamboyant gestures that do not serve to clarify the constant flow of communication. Though a conductor should not be limited in the actions he thinks necessary, a physical gesture on the podium which intrudes between the composer's creation and the audience cannot be justified. It has exceeded its function of musical communication. The audience should experience the interaction of the conductor, the orchestra and the composer's score, not the "conductor" as an isolated entity.

3 | *Authority and responsibility*

There is one point on which everyone concerned with an orchestral performance agrees. The conductor must have authority. However, authority is a diamond with many facets, and the conductor must know which facets of authority he should cultivate in order that he may best fulfill his function. In speaking of "authority," I use the term cultivate rather than assume because there is a vast difference between the obvious types of authority that can be assumed by the conductor or delegated to him, and the kind of authority that will gain for him the respect and full cooperation of his orchestra.

For example: the authority to select the members of his orchestra, the authority to arbitrarily dismiss them, the authority to choose only those compositions he feels will be most easily accomplished by the personnel he has, are some of the more obvious measures of authority desired by most conductors. But are they, or similar powers, the ones by which a conductor elicits from his players the willing submission that is so essential if the performance is to reflect his musical judgment?

There are three principal types of authoritative power commonly used by conductors to induce what they feel to be the kind of performance they want. These types are so clearly defined that the recognition of them almost serves to delineate three categories of conductors. First, the conductor who gets his results by virtue of the punitive power vested in him; the power to dismiss any player who might not contribute to an acceptable performance whether or not the conductor indicates or inspires it. In this situation, each player tries to perform as though he were in a chamber music ensemble, and together, they take on many of the responsibilities which normally belong to the conductor. They do this in self-defense, musically as well as economically. The conductor who relies on this power frequently lacks either the necessary musical scope or sufficient technical ability to guide his orchestra, and following his directions implicitly could lead to chaos.

Then there is an inordinately large number of conductors who exercise the force of their ego in the guise of authority. I do not mean an exaggerated manifestation of self-confidence, but an egotism born of the conductor's firm conviction that his often limited knowledge is all-encompassing; that fate has placed him in this position to enlighten the rest of mankind; and that technical requirements do not apply to him, but only to those who are there to do his bidding. He is generally supercilious, condescending, and prone to blame the orchestra for any misunderstanding of his direction. With this attitude, he does not really listen to the orchestra because he cannot conceive that the sounds would be other than those he hears in his mind. This kind of personality presents a challenge to his players, and they react by continually striving to prove themselves better rather than inferior to him. A performance so generated is usually superficial, sometimes brilliant, but very seldom emotionally satisfying.

The third, and smallest, group of conductors is the one that conducts with the authority of knowledge. They are much more introspective, more concerned with complete fulfillment of the composer's wishes, aware of the instrumentalists' capabilities, and approach the orchestra with respect for each individual as an important contributing element. Such a posture inspires the players to give of themselves unstintingly, and, in turn, infuses into the performance a spirit which transcends any problems that may exist in the physical execution on their part, or even possible lack of technical precision on the part of the conductor.

Standing above these three groups is the rare human being who can dominate his orchestra and audience with the combined authority of musical knowledge, understanding, and complete confidence that his technical facility is so highly developed he can communicate lucidly the most complicated or subtle utterances entrusted to him by the composer. Such a conductor fuses himself, the orchestra and the audience into one throbbing emotional entity, whirling in a mental centrifuge until no one is quite certain whether he is creator, performer or listener, yet feels as though he is a little of each.

| .... |

Any thought or discussion of authority must be coupled with a thought or discussion of responsibility. There can be no acceptable intelligent authority without responsibility. In law, a person who assumes an authority over something or someone, but who is himself incapable of understanding and assuming responsibility for the results of that authority, is considered incompetent. Also, the validity of one's authority is directly in proportion to the degree of responsibility he is ready to accept. This applies as much to artistic endeavor as it does to our social relationships. Inasmuch as it is agreed that a conductor must have authority, it follows then that he must be prepared to assume full responsibility for the results obtained through the use of that authority, and must know what it is he is responsible for, as well as to whom he owes this responsibility.

It may be an oversimplification to state, as I have in

the previous section, that the conductor is responsible *for* and *to* the orchestra and the composition he is performing. The true depth of such liability cannot be realized without an examination of the entire process that culminates in the re-creation of a composer's expression. It is an extremely long and involved process which begins before the composer is born and may end only when the last member of the audience has forgotten every sound. Even then it may not be finished, for some listeners might speak to others of their personal reaction to the music, and, in this manner, continue the wave effect.

Without delving too deeply beneath the surface, certain interesting points in this process merit special attention. Every composition is the result of generations of composers whose compounded efforts, dreams, frustrations and other influences have contributed to our musical evolution. The resources of each player reflect his own knowledge, the wisdom of his teachers and of those who came before them. Even the inanimate instruments on which they perform evolved through hundreds or thousands of years of discovery, experimentation and improvement. All of this is at the service of the conductor, and for the intelligent use thereof he must accept responsibility.

A modern symphony orchestra, in itself, is an awe-inspiring medium. It is seen as a group of people who have acquired an ability to read the musical notation and play upon certain readily available instruments—

routinely expected to be present and perform on cue as though, together, they made up a mechanical device. In actual fact, there is a great deal more to an orchestra than meets the eye. Deriving from the cultures of many civilizations, it is the most responsive, the most satisfying and, above all, the most forgiving instrument one can have.

If an instrumentalist should, through carelessness, incompetence or unavoidable accident, place his finger upon the wrong key or string, or blow improperly, his instrument will give forth a wrong sound beyond recall. On the other hand, since the strings, keys, pipes and reeds of a conductor's instrument are the minds of men, they will subconsciously evaluate the movement of his hands or other directions, and, if he allows them any intelligent privilege at all, they will correct in performance any of his indications which seem out of context with the composer's notation in their parts. Thus the orchestra takes upon itself a share of responsibility—but will continue to do so only as long as the conductor brings to the cooperative effort knowledge, concern, technical ability, and the musical integrity to which every good musician is dedicated. It is imperative, therefore, for everyone to realize the importance of a responsibility not only for the orchestra, but, more importantly, to the orchestra.

The study of and obedience to the music he performs and the obligation to include the audience as an active element are integral parts of the all-encompassing responsibility one must accept when he takes his place on the podium to exercise the proper authority and function of a conductor.

4 | *Burden of proof*

There may be some question as to the relevancy of the term "burden of proof" to the theme of this book, but the reasoning given here will remove any uncertainty. The foregoing chapters have shown that the podium behavior of a conductor is affected by the state of mind with which he approaches the task of communication with his orchestra. We have seen that his attitude is the sum of his judgment, acceptance of his function, honest desire to be understood, sense of timing, authority and responsibility, plus a fair evaluation of the role and contribution of the orchestra. It is this last item, the role the orchestra plays and its contribution to the ultimate result that is extremely significant, and involved in our reasoning at this point.

The physical force and volatile nature of an orchestra make it imperative that the conductor become as intimately familiar with it as he is with his own anatomy. In the act of conducting, he is called upon to exercise command of this equipment just as positively as he controls the muscles of his body, with corresponding responsibility for the truth of its actions. But even this may not be enough. The conductor must also be prepared with *proof*, at least in his own mind, that what he is asking the orchestra to say is the intent of the composer. Not presumptive opinion, but evidence that can be spelled out clearly or seen in the authority of the score. In assuming this premise, he is, in effect, acknowledging the existence of a "burden of proof."

In the creation of a composer's musical structure by a symphony orchestra under the leadership of a conductor, where does this "burden of proof" lie? That is the first and most important fact we must seek out, understand thoroughly, and believe implicitly before attempting to appraise the art of conducting. It is really a simple question that should have a direct one-word answer. Composer? Orchestra? Or conductor? Is a bad performance due to bad writing on the part of the composer, poor command of their instruments by the players, or wrong direction on the part of the conductor? And who, of these three, is to judge what is good? Let us examine the possibilities.

Through the years, the meaning of "burden of proof" has been variously expressed by many great conductors as it applied to their own approach and concept of responsibility. None said it better than the legendary Arturo Toscanini who has been alternately called, "angelic genius" and "satanic tyrant." I had the privilege of discussing the psychological aspects of conducting with this great man, and when I asked him what he considered the most important facet of a conductor's attitude, he answered me directly and simply. "If you want to be a conductor in the fullest sense of the word," he said, "you must keep one thing foremost in your mind. There are no good or bad orchestras; only good or bad conductors."

Certainly, Toscanini did not naïvely believe that all players were equally capable, or every orchestra equally good. Nor was he even facetiously suggesting any such possibility. He was dramatically pointing up one of the governing factors of the vital conductor-to-orchestra relationship. In effect, he was saying that, first and foremost, the conductor must realize that the burden of proof rests with him. Any attempt to shift this burden or blame will lead him to lower his demands on himself and weaken his integrity as a result.

| •••• |

Almost always, the conductor chooses the composition. Rarely is the procedure reversed. Theoretically, at least, the conductor chooses the orchestral players. If he doesn't select them personally, he generally has the authority to dismiss them if they prove incapable. Certainly the orchestra players are not allowed the freedom of criticizing or overruling the conductor, and many times the composer is not alive to interfere. He has had his say when he put his thoughts on paper and entrusted it to the conductor. In addition to this unchallenged control over the administrative elements, the conductor has one more intangible but invaluable force working in his favor—the love of music and pride of accomplishment that stimulate each player to do his utmost toward a good performance.

Unfortunately, the attitude displayed by many conductors reflects a seeming ignorance of these factors that are so much in his favor, though untold numbers of performances have been possible only because of them. There are some conductors who retain their positions, despite such ignorance, principally by their personal social grace plus the innate pride and ability of the orchestra. Hardly a goal to aim at, but this situation must be recognized for what it is, in order to establish an intelligent approach to the conductor's post.

The faults are not created by these conductors. At worst, it can be said they are willing victims; victims of misconceptions that have grown through the stages of theory, tradition and wishful thinking to the point of general acceptance.

Early in his musical studies, the student encounters seemingly authoritative statements such as: "Conduct-

ing cannot be taught"—"Conducting is instinctive"—
"You are either born with the ability to conduct or you
just can't do it"—"It has to be in you"—etc. I say "seemingly authoritative" because they are uttered by people
the student usually respects. The point that escapes him
is that all these statements have one thing in common.
They are opinions, not facts. As opinions they cannot be
proved or disproved, nor is it required that they be. But
opinions put forth quite honestly as such by persons of
recognized rank often take on the aura of fact, and
through lack of more comprehensive knowledge are accepted as fact by a large segment of the musical community.

Perhaps the complexity of the art makes it difficult to
fit into a known or prescribed pattern of teaching. Perhaps the human relations factor, the psychological
adjustments and the musical-technical preparation cannot all be successfully transmitted through any one man
or any specific system of education. That does not prove
it cannot be taught. If people can be taught the science
of psychiatry, the conductor's psychological thought
processes can be stimulated and directed. If young people can be trained to coordinate their muscles, limbs and
reflexes for a variety of sports, the conductor can also be
trained physically for his job. If pilots can be trained to
anticipate and correct problems while flying at 2500
miles an hour, a conductor can be developed with the
same skills for any known musical tempo. All these
things are known to be difficult, but accepted as, at least,

possible. Besides, who is to say that because he does not know how an art can be taught, therefore, the art cannot be learned. The determination to master an art, insofar as it is a reflection of a student's over-all attitude, dictates the degree of possibility. True progress begins when those who wish to conduct accept the burden of learning, the burden of curiosity, and, in effect, the burden of proof.

Because it governs the conductor's attitude toward the music, the orchestra, and to his own search for knowledge, we should examine the matter of "burden of proof" a bit further. In law, designation of the party upon whom the burden of proof falls is set by a very involved judicial process; because the establishment of legal authority is dependent upon opinion, understanding and interpretation of the tangible written word together with the intangible intent that may be implied. In music, the same elements are present. The tangible specific notation of the composer, and the intangible opinion of that notation as understood by the musician. The conductor facing a large group of people, each with his own personal opinion, must, therefore, immediately establish in his mind just where the burden of proof lies.

| •••• |

In the area of personal relationship between the conductor and the members of his orchestra, there are also conflicting theories. One, that social intimacy or personal friendship between conductor and players leads to a lessening of respect for the conductor. This belief has been widespread and carried to ridiculous extremes. I know one conductor, for example, who married a girl who formerly had been a player in his orchestra, and immediately forbade her to see or fraternize with the other members (of the symphony) who had been her friends for a long time. Naturally, his own personal relationship with the musicians is somewhat less than cordial, but I have found no evidence to indicate that this attitude has created or increased the orchestra's respect for him as a conductor.

On the other hand, the theory of complete social and personal equality in and out of the concert hall may have flaws as well. Conductors who come up out of the orchestra and have to face the same people with whom they formerly played are hard put to find a level of approach that would bridge the gap. They do not want to appear too authoritative lest their motives be suspect, while they do not want to be too lenient for the same reason. This can lead to serious problems, and require a long period of adjustment.

Any difficulties in the application of either theory are attributable to one cause: the degree to which the individual has failed to prepare himself as a conductor.

The orchestral musician has the right to and does expect no less from the conductor than the conductor expects for him. With confidence in his ability, no conductor need concern himself with a theory of personal relationship. If, in addition, he brings to the rehearsal integrity and humility, he will be admired and respected whether he encourages personal friendship with his players, or lives the life of a hermit.

Of necessity, the social relationship between conductor and orchestra, while working, is a very intimate one. Yet many conductors do their utmost to discourage any sociability, and even preach a doctrine of class distinction in the name of good discipline. The history of music is replete with legends of famous conductors whose tyrannical powers kept their players in constant fear and awe of them, thereby creating memorable performances. There are also reminiscences of conductors who were so nice, polite and understanding, that the orchestra, to use the vernacular, "walked all over them."

With these legends, many distorted with time, in his mind, the under-equipped or superficial personality arrives at the conviction that the first and most important part of a conductor's equipment is an ability to show the orchestra—"who's the boss." It is a premise that is easy to accept because it seems to provide a powerful and acceptable weapon which can help bolster the feeling of security so necessary for a conductor. That this is not based on fact—that the tyranny attributed to great conductors is not tyranny at all, but only the emotional outbursts of strong conviction—does not concern those who are desperately in need of even borrowed security. They welcome it in the false belief that, if *command* is the key, then the orchestra bears the burden of proof in performance; exposing an evasion by the conductor of at least some measure of responsibility.

Pursuing this thought into practical application, if the conductor chooses to believe that the burden of proof lies in the orchestra, he has only to approach a group with dignity and command them to play correctly and well. Then, if the results are not as anticipated, what could be more natural than to demand of the orchestra, "Why?" Asking himself the same question would immediately nullify this entire theory, and with such self-examination would evaporate the conductor's false security of assumed precedent.

As a result, the transcript of a typical rehearsal would contain far more questions asked by the conductor than corrections and advice given. In fact, a survey made at rehearsals of various metropolitan, community and amateur orchestras revealed a remarkable and surprising similarity in the words used by each conductor in his attempts to achieve his musical objective.

In almost every instance, when the conductor stopped his orchestra, he began by saying, "Why."

"Why don't you follow me?"
"Why don't you play together?"
"Why don't you follow the soloist?"
"Why are you dragging?"
"Why are you playing so loud" or "so soft?"
"Why are you rushing?"
"Why don't you watch me?"
"What do you think I am here for?"

And since protocol and tradition prevent the players from truthfully answering these obviously rhetorical questions, the conductor solves everything by saying, "Let's try it again."—as though the mere act of repetition can solve or correct any problems which occur in a passage or section.

The next most frequently heard remarks are slightly more positive. They always begin with "Don't."

"Don't hold back."

"Don't rush."

"Don't play so loud."

"Don't ignore the dynamics."

"Don't accent the wrong note." etc., etc.

And generally, again followed by the words, "Let's try it again." Then, of course, the most disturbing, the classic of inanities is heard all too often when the conductor stops the orchestra, sagely shakes his head from side to side, and says, "Something is wrong, let's try it again."

About the only variation on this use of generalities is the remark that begins with "You must."

"You must follow me."

"You must play together."

"You must play the right notes."

"You must pay attention," and so on.

Ironically, in practically every instance when playing was resumed after such a comment, the conductor did exactly the same thing with his hands as he had previously done. In this manner, I have heard the same mistakes and the same comments made over and over again until, in apparent disgust, the conductor would say to the orchestra, "It's no use, you just can't do it."

Other specific instances to which I have been a witness can serve further to bring home to the aspiring conductor the importance of accepting the "burden of proof." During one rehearsal, the Russian Easter Overture of Rimsky-Korsakoff was being prepared. This overture begins with a chanting theme written in 5/2 metre with various sections of the orchestra making their entrances within the principal beats. After numerous stops, several "Why don't you-s" and "You must-s," all before they reached the fifth measure, the conductor said quite seriously, "This is the only way I was taught to conduct five to a measure, and that's the only way I know, so you will just have to get it from my beat. I really can't understand why you don't come in properly." Coming from a conductor who had already had his own orchestra for several years, it was much more than an obviously useless and ill-advised remark. It was a manifestation of his basic attitude toward an understanding of the conductor-to-orchestra relationship. Or perhaps lack of understanding would describe it more aptly.

A more graphic example is the true story of the conductor who had been making the musicians miserable with his vague and unrelated gestures for some time. Orchestral players, as a rule, are a long suffering, obedient lot, but this was too much. In desperation, one of the wind players rose and asked, "Maestro, please, couldn't you clarify your beat a little, or at least give us a cue for

our entrance?" Whereupon the conductor angrily re-
plied, "What kind of a musician are you that you want
me to give you a beat and a cue? Can't you see I am busy
conducting?"

These anecdotes may seem like an exaggeration not
worth the attention given them here—it might be so if
these were isolated instances. But this method and approach is used so consistently throughout the orchestral
society that it has taken on the character of a serious
mental concept of accepted rehearsal procedure.

The attitude born of the belief that the conductor has
his chores to do while at the same time the orchestra has
its job—both working simultaneously and parallel with
each other—develops out of ignorance, not ignorance of
the theory or practice of music, but the ignorance of
who must carry the heaviest burden in the relationship
between conductor and orchestra.

A conductor must know that he cannot "fool" any
orchestra at any time. If he is incompetent, vague, or
concerns himself more with his personal effect on the
audience than on the orchestra, the players are acutely
aware of it, though the audience and even some music
critics are not. A creditable performance is not always
proof that the conductor is good, regardless of the credit
given him by audience or critic. By the same token, if a
performance is noticeably bad, the fault does not necessarily lie with the orchestra, as is so often thought. Re-
grettably, many concert reviewers lack the awareness of
this, and tend to praise the conductor for good results

and condemn the orchestra for bad. They generally do it politely by saying the orchestra was ragged and could have used more rehearsal, and the conductor who does not assume the full burden of proof takes comfort and assumes justification of himself from such reviews.

But, can the orchestra's seeming deficiencies be the real reason for unsuccessful results? What about the conductor's authority over the orchestra? Is it or isn't it his responsibility to do everything necessary in order to insure cohesion and musicality?

One very highly regarded conductor, justly famous for the beauty of sound he always elicited, insisted everyone observe his beat carefully. And he did provide a clear beat. On the other hand, his most often repeated remark to his very fine orchestra was, "Don't play like machines. You are all individuals with a heart and talent. Play with your own heart and musical taste. Not mechanically." Who is to blame, if occasionally there is less than precision in performance? The orchestra, trying to do as their conductor asked, or the conductor who perhaps allowed the individual freedom of emotion to interfere with the ensemble accuracy? This is not a question of musical right or wrong. It is another consideration in determining where the burden of proof lies.

Actually, except with very fine conductors, the often insufficient rehearsal time is sometimes used more for the conductor's benefit than for that of the orchestra. After all, the players were auditioned and it was determined that they had the ability to read well at sight, and knew the orchestral repertoire before the rehearsal. If there is subsequently a consistent roughness, poor sound balance, rhythmic insecurity, etc., it is more of an indication that perhaps the conductor was not sufficiently prepared. Can a conductor really think, then, that a poor performance is primarily the orchestra's fault? Perhaps the uninformed listener cannot know the answer, but the orchestra can and does. *Therefore, the conductor must.*

However, as obvious as this is, there has been much shifting of blame, or burden of proof, from the conductor to the orchestra. The ignorance and conceit of the conductors who live by and propagate this theory of "Conductor—good; Orchestra—bad," have given rise to a story widely circulated among orchestral musicians all over the world. It is about the conductor who constantly blamed his orchestra for not playing as he was conducting. The orchestra held a meeting to discuss what might be done about this, and elected a spokesman to speak to the conductor. He said quite calmly and politely, "Maestro, the orchestra is very concerned with the music as you are conducting it, but if you don't stop your abuse of us, we promise to follow you implicitly." It seems they made their point.

An orchestra is a most willing instrument. It wants to be directed. The players want to submit to the conductor because they are aware of their need for him. But because of their knowledge they cannot be blind, and will not trust themselves completely to a leader who has less than wide, comprehending vision.

He who would approach the podium must accept the condition that the burden of proof rests with him, and if his attitude reflects this belief, all the forces involved in creating a musical performance will combine to reflect his image.

5 | *Preparation*

As I have mentioned previously, the ideal preparation for the study of the art of conducting should include several years of experience as an orchestral musician, playing at least one instrument of each section with various conductors and under every possible set of circumstances; in large and small auditoriums, with different seating arrangements, stages that have various acoustical problems, and open-air as well as indoor concerts; becoming familiar with the orchestral repertoire of every period as seen through the minds of conductors with widely divergent backgrounds.

But why? Why is this so important or necessary? Must a conductor be able to actually play each part in order to have a proper grasp of its problems and demands? Or is it to prove that he knows as much or more than anybody else involved? The answer to the last two questions, strangely enough, is "No." While the great value of such ability, experience and knowledge gained is beyond question, the skills themselves are secondary. The principal reason is to learn at first hand just what the player cannot do himself and what is needed by him in the way of guidance from the podium. For, we must remember, one of the prime reasons for having a conductor is to provide that which the players cannot provide for themselves. Also, the psychological understanding of the best orchestra-to-conductor relationship can be acquired more easily by experiencing over and over again the need for, and often the lack of, clearly delineated directions from the podium.

Where the opportunity for such personal participation is not available, an alternative might be to observe for a long time and question many players, without prejudice. It is hard, though, to accept the frustration of others as our own. There is a tendency to assume some measure of exaggeration when a player lists his problems or grievances against one or another conductor. However, a sincere endeavor to find the truth will result in the eventual conviction that the frustrations are not personal, but general. And because they are general, they must be of concern to all conductors.

No one denies the value of preparation through participation. Every responsible music educator agrees that a good way to become familiar with the orchestra is to be an integral part of it. Therefore, we may assume that the experience gained through being several parts of this highly involved human instrument is undoubtedly even better. Logic beyond contradiction? It would seem so. However, in reality, what appears to be an incontrovertible fact is actually one side of a paradox.

Despite the universal agreement regarding the importance and value of such preparation, only a small percentage of conservatories and universities offering conducting courses make this experience an absolute requirement. Naturally, in view of this, the student can rationalize and convince himself that all the years of work toward orchestral familiarity is not quite as necessary as it seems. Besides, in almost every conducting course, an equivalent is acceptable to meet the requirements.

The equivalent accepted in most cases is "observation." One is expected to have spent a minimal time sitting in an orchestra or attending rehearsals as an observer. It is taken for granted that the time so spent will provide first-hand knowledge of all the instruments, their relationships with each other and the conductor, the human reflex factor, the psychological barriers and sympathies of all concerned, and the myriad other subtle elements of ensemble activity. Sometimes, six weeks at a summer school dominated by a major orchestra, or a few weeks of lectures and discussions at the summer home of a famous conductor, are considered sufficient preparation for advanced study of the conductor's art. In some cases, this all too limited exposure is believed to provide enough qualification for a professional conducting position.

Surely, such experience cannot take the place of intense personal participation, nor can it provide even a reasonable facsimile of true orchestral life. The acceptance of this equivalent, however, encourages many to compromise in preparing for a career, with the expectation that they will be able to acquire the needed insight in their later experience.

But just what is being given up or postponed in this compromise? *Without knowing what it is,* not having experienced it, *how can it be sought later on?*

To admit that any part of the necessary training is being by-passed is to admit lack of preparation. To admit lack of preparation is to admit, at least, some incompetence. How, then, can one who is admittedly less than fully competent qualify for a conducting assignment during which he hopes to learn that which he should have known before picking up the baton? The logical answer would seem to be, "He can't." But among conductors, and teachers of the craft, there are those who believe it is not fashionable to be logical about so supposedly illogical a subject.

In some circles, even to consider conducting as a "craft" is viewed as heresy. Why, if the requirements and mechanics of conducting could have a logical sequence and definition, what would happen to the mystical powers only conductors are presumably born with? A conductor might then be no more privileged than a pianist, violinist, cellist or other instrumentalist. He could be held completely responsible for everything that emanates from his instrument just as they are, and his faults of technique or musicianship would be similarly exposed.

So, the myth of a special type of human being, who is a "born conductor," is perpetuated by indeterminate or varying requirements and standards for even competitive evaluation. In addition, we are told that conducting is an art form so personal as to defy explanation, responsibility and criticism.

There can be no doubt that the art of conducting is very personal. But so is every other art form. It is art precisely because it is personal. However, the means of communication within any art form—the craftsmanship or technique—cannot be a purely personal matter if it is to succeed in its purpose. In projection, art utterances always involve more than one person. At the very least, two people must be familiar with the physical means of communication, the projector and the receiver.

No two instrumentalists play exactly alike. This is the personal element of their art. But the technique or facility with which they display their art has a common basis that can be recognized and evaluated, if only by comparison. And, too, this technique is expected of them as a prerequisite to artistic expression.

The conductor, on the other hand, enjoys an unearned

privilege—a double-edged one, in fact. His instrument will often correct his mistakes and conceal his technical deficiency, or when this is impossible, it can be burdened with the blame. If the orchestral player would react to a conductor's technique as truthfully as the keys do to a pianist's fingers, every conductor would, in short order, know what he must do as well as how he must think. This is why it is so vitally important for a conductor to have experienced the reactions he will hope to stimulate in others; to have learned through personal experience the kind of help a player actually needs, when and why, to know what the players cannot do without help. From this experience comes an applicable version of the golden rule.

The conductor, when he faces an orchestra after having played in one, knows he should do for the players those things which he himself had looked for when he was among them—the things which, in deliberate and consistent use, constitute the technique of conducting.

6 | *Technique*

For a long time, there has existed a widespread theory that the art of conducting and the technique of conducting are separate skills. It is also generally accepted that, to conduct, one must have an innate talent, qualities of leadership, etc., and if one also managed to achieve a mechanical dexterity, well and good. Again and again, we are told a conductor must know his music, must understand the composer, must be able to "interpret" a score, and if he can qualify in all this, communication will follow.

It is undeniably true a conductor must know his music, understand the composer, be able to interpret the score, but this is just as true of every other musician. The one single thing which distinguishes one musician from another is the physical manner in which he expresses his knowledge: with hands and feet at an organ; with lips on a wind instrument; with manipulations of sticks, mallets, hammers and fingers on percussion instruments; or the intelligible patterns described in the air by the conductor.

Clearly then, the particular skill needed to control an instrument or group of instrumentalists is the element of any musician's art which determines whether he is a pianist, violinist, other instrumentalist, or a conductor. A musicologist also has the knowledge and understanding of a performer, but his medium of expression is the written or spoken language of his choice. In this, too, he must have a facility comparable to that of a player. How can anyone, therefore, minimize the importance of this requirement!

All who perform as musicians must be endowed with similar talents for introspection, projection and education, for their role is the same. Each may develop several physical skills, and as a result, be capable of expressing himself on different instruments, or, as a conductor in addition to playing an instrument. However, one kind of muscular development cannot serve in place of the other, and none are interchangeable. Otherwise, any musician who could play one instrument would automatically be able to play any other, or, without additional training, conduct an orchestra.

There is little doubt about the specific physical requirements for the various instruments because their peculiarities have been known for a long time. The art of conducting is a comparatively new one, growing imperceptibly at first from the Kapellmeister who directed as he played, to a human metronome who beat the tempo with a stick on the floor, to the early opera conductor who worked to keep singers and orchestra together, up to the present highly complicated function it has become.

It will help to place the conductor's technique in a better perspective if we look back and compare the causes or reasons for this technique with those for instrumental techniques. In the case of all instruments, the position of the hands and body, while articulating the keys, strings, valves, tone holes, etc., was dictated by the physical structure, size, shape and other characteristics indigenous to each one. This forced the player to adjust himself to it, and create a pattern of motion that would make possible the execution of any musical expression known to him.

Most contemporary instruments were very crude in their early stages of development, but, at the same time, the musical demands on the player were rather limited. Subsequently, the instruments were improved to allow the players more comfortable movements so that, as music itself progressed and became more complicated and more demanding, the player had only to improve his original dexterity. The basic method of playing remained the same, determined by the instrument in greater measure than by the music.

However, in arriving at a method of communication as a conductor, there was no structural object that could determine even the question of whether to sit or stand, or where to do whatever it is a conductor was supposed to do. When a coordinating factor other than a player became desirable, each one (usually the composer) who undertook to carry out this function did so in his own way, subject to his own physical and musical limitations, much as very early composers used their individual method of notation. Since then, everything that has become the conductor's responsibility has been caused by the rhythmic, harmonic and dynamic development of composition. Now it is the simplicity or complexity of any given score that determines the facility needed by a conductor.

| .... |

Another comparison should be made in regard to the matter of technique. This time let us compare the mental attitude of the conductor with the state of mind considered perfectly natural by instrumentalists. Through common usage, the word "technique" has become synonymous with the purely physical action required in playing. With this has come an acceptance of the technique or physical action as a normal and necessary factor in performance. Yet the moment a musician decides to learn to conduct, he immediately becomes almost completely preoccupied with a fear of the word "technique." Even those who are accomplished instrumentalists and who know full well the importance of their technical facility, fall prone to this fear.

The unfounded fear is itself the result of misconceptions shared by conductors, players and members of their audience. Misconception of the meaning of technique—the belief that technique is synonymous with mechanical, or that technique means rigid conformity, or the belief that there is no specific source from which it is derived, that there is no authority for it, and that it cannot be learned or developed without the opportunity of conducting on a regular schedule. Once the fear is rationalized by the acceptance of these misconceptions as fact, it is evaded, made non-existent. It becomes easier to say that conducting technique as a prerequisite is not absolutely necessary.

It is imperative that the misconceptions responsible for the fear of technique be corrected before one can begin to understand the use and value thereof. When this is done, it will be possible to seek out the basis and logic of technique in conducting.

Is technique a mechanical, restrictive device? Or is it a necessary physical adjunct that gives substance to "art?" The root of technique is the Greek word *"Techne,"* which means *"art."* From the dictionary, we learn that "technic" is *"The method of performance or manipulation in any art"*; also, "technique" means *"The practical details or methods by which an artist in any*

line expresses his mental conceptions." Art, as we already know, encompasses a system of rules for the accomplishment of an intelligent purpose. Technique,
then, is a means by which to carry out an artistic idea,
subject to the rules necessary for its purpose. Only the
application of physical motion, or technique, can transform the conductor's mental concept of the score into a
living entity, into a musical utterance that can be heard
and provoke an emotional reaction. Technique is thus
not a choice of method within the art of conducting, but
it is the art itself. The only question remaining is how
well to develop this art, and not whether to develop it.
By now it should be clear, that without a well-controlled
intelligible dexterity (technique) there is no art except
in the mind of the artist.

| •••• |

Accepting the inevitable conclusion that art is not manifest without technique, what about the fear of conformity in the execution of the technique? This seems to
worry young conductors more than the intricacies of the
music they hope to perform. For the answer, we can turn
to nature and the physiology of the human animal. With
only a very elemental knowledge of anatomy, it must be
evident that physical conformity is almost impossible to
achieve. Those who fear it so much would have to devote many years to special exercise before they could
claim conformity of action with any other person, always

running the risk of becoming a caricature of the person being imitated.

A student trying to emulate his teacher or idol, however fine he may be, would appear as awkward and ineffective as a stout person five feet tall trying to walk with the same gait as someone over six feet tall and very thin. The natural law governing man's use of his legs is the same for all, but individual physical characteristics conspire to establish a personal use for each one. Such factors as length of the leg (dictating length of stride), body weight (dictating speed and resilience), and muscular coordination vary with every person. Thus, there are as many styles of walking as there are people, while, on the surface, the act of walking appears to conform more rigidly to a physical pattern than anything else we do. It is, at the same time, the most similar and most widely different action of individual men.

The upper part of the body, more intimately involved in conducting, is governed by the same natural laws with much wider latitude of motion, allowing greater freedom. Here, too, the motions of the arms, shoulders and head are governed by weight, size, muscular development and coordination. These are the factors that make it impossible for two people to conduct exactly alike, even though they may deliberately set out to use the same gestures.

Examined in this light, it is obvious one does not become a conformist or give up individual personality by developing a specific physical form of communication.

Conductors need not be afraid of looking like one another on the podium, nor should they waste time and effort trying not to look like someone else. Once this fear of regimentation is removed from a conductor's mind, a vast area of unending variation in the application of the technique to his musical expression opens up for him.

| .... |

With the fear of restriction by technique eliminated, there still remains the question—is it the whole of the art, or only one of several techniques that combine to make up the art? If it is only one of several, what is its comparative value, and why?

As far as the conductor is concerned, the physical motion is the culmination or end result of a long, involved process. A continuing process beginning with the reading of a score, comprehension of its intent, determination of the necessary requirements from the orchestra, decision as to best procedure for the purpose, and finally, the action itself to communicate this to the orchestra. A chain of mental activity, inseparably forged to the physical motion which is only one link, the link through which the entire chain can become visible, the link through which the orchestra is permitted to see into the mind of the conductor. While for the conductor the motion is the end of the chain, to the orchestra it is the beginning and basis for another highly involved mental and physical process. Each player must read the music, comprehend its intent in accordance with the light shed by the conductor, decide on procedure and execute physically.

This makes two chains of procedure, but neither is all inclusive or sufficient unto itself. Neither contains an actual beginning or end, and neither fragment of chain is the beginning or the end of the complete chain. The total activity of the conductor, mental and physical, is only a part of a longer sequence, one that begins before he injects himself, and continues on after he has made his contribution. Even the composer's work is not the beginning of the chain, since his knowledge and ideas are derived from sources outside of himself. The score, a tangible representation of his thought process, is entrusted to the conductor who must illuminate it for the orchestra to reflect.

If the light shed by the conductor is dim, due to the weakness of either a mental or physical link in this chain, the reflection as presented by the orchestra will be correspondingly vague or distorted.

At the other end, the audience is not the final link. There remain the effects of emotional reaction, actions which might be started or stimulated by the music, and, if nothing else, the memory that cannot be erased.

Even the analogy of a chain, and the undeniable premise that a chain is as strong as its weakest link, cannot sufficiently describe the inter-relationship and equal importance of the mental and physical processes in conducting. They are as closely tied as a man with his shadow or his mirrored image. We cannot arbitrarily set a value on the "technique" itself any more than we can dictate that our mirror reflect something intended, but invisible. Accordingly, the movements or "technique" must be developed and polished to the highest degree in order to achieve the most definitive reflection.

By the laws of physics, the brilliance of a mirrored reflection is determined by the illumination of the object to be mirrored; not by the amount of light cast on the mirror itself. Because of this, the conductor must realize there can be no flaw in his section of the chain, for it will be reflected. He cannot allow the separation of his mental concepts from his physical proficiency, for one does not exist without the other. He must be aware that the so-called "technique" is not a thing apart to be used or not, that the physical motion is the manifestation of his thoughts. Therefore, it is an inseparable part of *all those things, which, in deliberate and consistent use, constitute the art of conducting.*

7 | *Source and substance*

At the very moment when we accept the inevitability of a physical format as the primary link between the conductor and orchestra, additional questions arise. What is the source of the pattern? Where do we find authority for it, and why are there different patterns?

The various texts describing and picturing the essentials of conducting are all generally valid. They stem from exhaustive studies of past conductors, experimentation and, to some extent, from personal preference and convenience. Some go further and provide instruction in the application of traditional patterns to specific compositions. But for the most part, they are concerned with the substance (technique) and its use, rather than the source.

However, without a conscious realization of the source which is, in itself, the authority, some conductors fail to understand the reason and logic of technique. Consequently, they ignore it, or use only as much of it as can be easily accomplished by them. Whatever they then lack in communicative ability, they try to make up through persuasive personality, ego, economic power or sheer force of will. A surprising number of regularly employed conductors fall into this category.

I could name the source—in one word—and wait while the surprised reader exclaims: "Certainly! but everyone knows that!" Perhaps so. Perhaps they did know and have forgotten, or if they do know, it is possible they do not really believe it. If it is true everyone knows the source, it appears a well guarded secret, judging from the way so many conductors choose to ignore it by failing to cultivate their art accordingly. On the other hand, it may be that conductors are as human as anyone else, and tend, as we all do, to underestimate the value of something we take for granted. Whatever the reason, a new search for the "familiar" source may reveal a forgotten value or a new understanding of its force.

| •••• |

Looking through the archives and tracing back through history is a slow and tedious process fraught with many dangers, such as the danger of unearthing a theory which may or may not be correct, or of finding scraps of unrelated information that would have to be sorted and checked for plausibility and feasibility before they could be accepted or applied.

For the adventure of discovery, let us instead put aside our histories of conducting, handbooks on the art, and try to forget what has been said about the subject. To grasp the conductor's function deductively, so to speak, we posit a situation in which there are composers and orchestras enjoying each other's cooperation, but there is as yet no conductor. Now, suddenly, you are projected into the picture and asked to conduct. You are required to establish a craft where none has existed before; to transform the composer's symbols into readily intelligible motions without consultation and without the opportunity for explanation. What would you do?

To what or to whom can you turn? The composer, as a person, ceased to exist when he relinquished the score to you. Beyond what he wrote, he can be of no further help. His communication was fully and clearly stated in musical notation, a code or language you are expected to read easily with complete comprehension. The orchestra cannot help, because not one of the players possesses or has the knowledge of all the inter-related parts of the composition. In fact, that is why they require a conductor. So you are left alone to find a way.

How to begin? You cannot start by stamping your foot. That method is too noisy and far too limited. Your head is movable, but wagging it about might inhibit sharp thinking. And bowing continuously from the waist could be very cumbersome. This leaves only the arms and hands to work with. How fortunate! The most highly developed, most variably jointed, most flexible and most sensitive extremities are available for you to use. By a special stroke of luck, they are placed high on the body where they can be more easily seen by the orchestra. All in all, the most logical choice for conducting.

Am I being facetious? Certainly. But isn't this the point at which the same surprised reader should jump up and ask, "If the position and movement of the arms and hands have been apparent since the origin of man, and they are so logically the most appropriate limbs for conducting, how is it they were not considered in the first place?" A partial answer is that the seemingly obvious is not necessarily the most readily seen. That which is clearly understood is much more easily recognized. However, the principal reason for ignoring the obvious (the use of the hands and arms) is the early belief that the conductor was to be a non-playing functionary who should not be seen, lest he divert the attention of the audience. Needless to say, this phase passed quite quickly.

What we know today to be the functions and responsibilities of the conductor suggested themselves one at a time, each additional function almost an outgrowth of the previous one rather than different branches. When the ensemble lost its feeling of intimacy, the first requirement was for someone to beat the time, so they could continue to play together despite the increased distance from each other. Then came the attempt of the conductor to control tonal values for the sake of clarity; thus utilizing both hands—one for the beat, and the other for the volume balance. And, for a while, the conductor served this way in a more or less utilitarian capacity.

In the course of time, composers began to deviate from their formal section writing in which changes in color were made by entrances of a group at a time— woodwinds; strings; brass. In this type of structure, with the stylized harmonic movements of the period, players did not have to rely on themselves entirely for their entrances. They could almost know in advance how many measures to count, and if they lost count, they could merely follow the example of another member of their section. Or they could listen for the expected inevitable harmonic resolution or cadence.

As composers went on to separate the blocks of colors into shades and tints by using each instrumental color and character individually, the player's problems became more complicated. No longer could he rely on someone else to count for him, nor could he depend upon the chord sequence. The harmonic progressions became less and less helpful in maintaining his place. In addition, the continuous advancement of musical freedom placed additional burdens upon the player. He had to read and play more difficult material, concentrate intently to count a greater variety of rhythmic divisions, adjust his intonation to new intervals and balances, and cope with new concepts of line and thought. At the same time, he was expected to hear every voice, recognize the over-all activity into which he must fit his part, and be responsible for emotional quality of the sounds he made.

No wonder the players sought help. The conductor was already in their sight, so it was to him they turned. Quite logically! As each new problem presented itself, the conductor was invited to share the responsibility for its solution. While his first duties were to supervise tempo and balance, it was felt he could help further. Reading the score, he could keep track of each line and indicate the entrances in the event a player lost count. Then he was asked to help delineate the rhythmic complications, help the players visualize the phrases; in general, help them to understand the essence of the music which had become too involved for them to grasp from their position.

The emphasis is on the word "help." This is the key to the conductor's function and responsibility. Never did a player, or group of players, ask the conductor to take over any one of their duties. They merely, justifiably, asked him to help them carry out the intent of the composer as disclosed in the score.

In acceding to their request for help, as it became necessary, the conductor also accepted the responsibility for the continuance of such help. The orchestras assumed it would continue, and concentrated their efforts toward improving their instrumental facility. The composers assumed it, and, because of it, they felt free to create new thoughts, new intellectual complexities, and increase the rate of musical progress.

All this help is provided by the modern conductor through the substance of his "technique." To deny this help or any part of it now, for whatever theoretical reason, is like reneging on a promise to catch a man in a safety net after he has already jumped.

The conductor today is obliged to maintain the responsibility for stimulating the increasingly difficult and involved technique required by the music of our time. And as the modern instrumentalist must continually improve his facility, learn new fingerings, new tonal effects, and in some cases, entirely new ways of playing, the conductor is expected to follow suit. For, in electing to be a conductor, understanding all the word implies, he, in effect, promised to do so.

The contemporary composers write for orchestra with conductor, not merely for orchestra, as the titles suggest. The conductor's part in the composition has become as integral as the tuba part, violin part or any other instrument or section, because the composer took his (the conductor's) function into account in conceiving the work. If a commission were to specify a composition for orchestra without conductor, the composer would write differently, just as he would if he were told there could be no trombones or English horns or cellos. The forces available to him govern the technical scope employed by a composer, though not the musical or emotional expression.

We all know there is great music scored without certain instruments, and equally great music scored with them. But we wouldn't, for a moment, think of leaving out the trombones and tuba when performing Richard Strauss' "Don Juan" simply because the first symphony of Beethoven gets along magnificently without them. Similarly, if a composition is scored, as most contemporary works are, for orchestra with conductor, we cannot withhold the exact execution of the conductor's part because other compositions do not require it.

There is also the question of ability, or degree of ability, to cope with any given voice in a composition. The conductor is the first to point a finger if a player cannot or does not learn his part, and exercises the right to criticize and condemn the player for incompetence. The logical argument in his favor is, of course, that each part is a precise unit of a well-integrated whole and, if not played correctly, will not fit properly. Therefore, mediocrity cannot be condoned. True! But the same logic holds with regard to the conductor's part. Perhaps even more so. A deviation by a player usually has a momentary effect on the balance, harmony or rhythm, whereas a deviation by the conductor is like a stone cast into a pond. It creates ever-widening ripples of distortion, with almost unending effect on the music.

These are some of the reasons why the functions of the modern conductor are so complex and difficult to accomplish. Correspondingly, the same reasons make plain why his responsibilities are of such magnitude.

| .... |

But how does one begin? You have done so already. You know now what your role must be and why. You know you will have to do something, principally with your hands, to help the orchestra. With this knowledge, you are prepared to pursue the original question. Where is the source and authority for the substance needed to accomplish the conductor's commitment? The answer lies in the only possible place—the composer's score.

Every one of the "surprised readers" might say, "We knew it all the time." Is this true? If they did, why do the myths persist? If they believe there is a source with authority, why do many maintain that the act of conducting presupposes an assumed generally metaphysical insight and does not require the logic and reason of the art? Why do some go from teacher to teacher, and from country to country, in the hope of learning what and how to do that which a conductor is supposed to do, all the time carrying the scores in their pockets or looking at them with unseeing eyes? Why are there those who believe the only way is to watch or imitate the apparently successful? Or those who are satisfied they can learn by practicing prescribed patterns, or no patterns, to the sounds of a recorded performance; or those who are convinced that the only answer lies in having their own orchestra?

All of them, student and professional alike, have access to the same source and authority, yet few realize it. Each one, projected into the hypothetical situation described earlier, would have the answer to the questions, How does one begin?—Where can I look?—What is the source? They would have but to study the score carefully, not only to find out *what it says,* but to see *how the score speaks* as well.

How the score speaks is the clue to how the conductor speaks (physically). Even to the detail of whether the direction of a beat should be down or up. For the purpose of illuminating this fact, it would help to picture the most common method of modern notation. Basically, it is a system of measures—the lengths and divisions of which may be determined by the composers —separated by bar lines, which encompass the divisions or rhythmic patterns. This is the mold into which the composer chooses to pour his harmonic-melodic phrase mixture. It is a self-imposed restriction, as a matter of fact, since he is at liberty to reject this traditional method if he should so desire. He may divide his metres in any number of ways, but the purpose of the bar line remains the same—to separate the rhythmic frames within the work.

The conductor, charged to project each score as it is notated, must indicate the various pulses or beats as they have been placed between the bar lines—primarily to carry out his original duty to help maintain the tempo. Then, through a selected movement, he must heighten the players' awareness of the beginning of each rhythmic block (measure) so they will convey more definitely the divisions marked by the bar lines. Thus, in carrying out the instructions of the score in order to transmit the consciousness of the metre to the audience, the conductor bows to the authority of the score as the source of his technique.

There can be no denial of the score as the source and authority for that which the conductor should communicate to his players. This can almost be taken for granted. As to method, conductors and players have accepted the format prescribed in the textbooks and validated by tradition, with only some secondary reservations. At the very least, there is almost a universal agreement that the first beat—the one that indicates the beginning of a pulse pattern, and places the sound in relation to the bar line —should be indicated with a downward motion. Naturally, the last beat of each measure would consequently be indicated in an upward motion, with the intervening beats—when there are more than two in a measure— moving in directions which would conveniently position the hands for the repetition of the sequence.

Logical, simple, and elementary to the point of boredom? Why is it, then, that the most prevalent complaint by players—in symphony orchestras at every budget level, as well as in the so-called "commercial" ensembles —concerns this primary facet of a conductor's technique? What prompts highly skilled orchestral musicians to say, in exasperation, of some conductors, "If he would only give us a clear beat and leave us alone, we would do the rest."

Evidently, this "elementary" principle is not as elementary as we think. Perhaps the offending conductors concede the validity of it, take it for granted with the best intentions, and then for some unexplainable psychological reason, ignore it in practice. It may be for different reasons in each case. Some err because they do not really know the reason for their function, some because they are not fully aware of their function and responsibility; some deliberately choose to shift this function to the orchestra because of their inability to carry it out capably, and some feel this service is beneath them since they are dedicated to the aesthetic essence of the music.

Whatever the reason, the results are the same. Mediocre performance. Moreover, it indicates a lack of regard for the score as a source of their own authority. A conductor must go to the score (source) to find out how fast to beat, what divisions to emphasize, what phrasing, dynamics, colors, forms, emotion, drama have been created for him to translate. He cannot accept someone else's opinion, however pleasing, as to how the score speaks, or guess at what it might say. Unless he can, if necessary, show that what he asks the orchestra to do is spelled out or clearly implied by the composer's notation, he has no real authority, only a weakness most orchestras will quickly sense.

| • • • • |

WHY DOWN?   WHY UP?

Every conductor should be able to devise a method (substance or technique) for himself as if he were the first of his kind, and there were no texts or teachers to guide him. With an intelligent use of the same scores, as the source, the basic movements developed by each individual would be quite similar.

In order to learn why this would be so, we have to apply the instructions or intimations in the score to the sum of the forces we already have—instinct, knowledge, physical attributes, cognizance of our habits and the reaction they evoke in others. Complete effectiveness as a conductor depends, in great measure, upon conscious and subconscious relationships with others, with the last point possibly the most important one. Since it is necessary to create an instant sign language, we must relate the musical notation to a physical movement which will be immediately recognized as the most natural one for the intent. In order for a gesture to be so recognized, it should be one normally used to emphasize a similar intent in daily conversation, thus establishing a common point of reference. If a conductor is to be of help to the orchestra, he must avoid using an arbitrarily devised set of gestures whose meaning and intent may be clear only to himself.

The entire physical manifestation of conducting is made up of descriptive arm and hand movements which people in every walk of life have been using as far back as history can trace. They are the same gestures that make it possible for people, from different parts of the world and differing cultures, to make themselves understood though they do not know each other's spoken language. Just as it would in such personal conversation, a strong conviction of intent materially aids in the projection and purposeful accomplishment of the gesture.

To illustrate: One instance in which a descriptive gesture is invariably used in place of words is in the quick explanation of a spiral staircase. A person who is supercilious or insufficiently interested will merely lightly wiggle his hand from the wrist. Another, who sincerely wants you to know the object as he knows it, will take the trouble to use his arm as well as his hand, start at a low point and continue to raise his arm as the hand describes a spiral. The first, vaguer, gesture might have been misunderstood to mean a revolving staircase, while the second indicated the function of the stairway to reach from one level to another, leaving less margin for error of comprehension.

A comparable simile applies to the conductor, particularly with regard to his first obligation to establish tempo and rhythmic pattern. That type of conductor who, from Elysian heights, neglects to contribute his full share of energy and interest to the accurate presentation of the composer's musical forms, usually finds less than full delight in the pleasures he had hoped to enjoy therein.

As a more specific example, let us take the gesture with which we hope to indicate the first beat. In order to have identity, it must be unique. Also, it must have a quality that will mark it as the appropriate one to display the dominating pulse of the measure. The words "one" or "first" have always been indicated by holding a finger in a vertical attitude; accordingly, we choose a vertical motion. For emphasis, the most commonly used gesture is that of slamming the hand down on the nearest object; so we move the hand downward in a vertical motion. This direction and attitude of the first beat is another one of those things, "everybody knows." However, the realization that the movement stems directly from the method of musical notation is not quite so general.

The score, in effect, says: the first beat of each measure shall be identified as such (vertical attitude) for the purpose of proper rhythmic diction, and the identification shall be accomplished by emphasis in sound (downward motion) in order that the audience receive the musical intention through its aural senses. In this way, the score directs the pedantic execution of the beat.

Continuing, along these lines, to correlate the intent and purpose of the succeeding beats with gestures of known reference, the conductor can arrive at a practical form of communication homogeneous with his natural and developed attributes. He is thereby creating a technique, personal to himself, yet universally effective.

It is, certainly, helpful and intelligent to seek instruction and advice of others, but the reflected light of a teacher's knowledge and experience is wasted unless we use it to illumine our own search. This analysis was not intended to prove what we already know, that the first beat is downward because it is the strongest beat in the measure. The purpose is to point out the authority for this knowledge, for there are inumerable additional things a conductor must do within that same first beat if he is to express what is written, things for which there are no guidebooks, which must be accomplished differently from moment to moment, which depend entirely upon split-second judgment, and which are indicated, each time anew, in the only authoritative source—the score.

Within the one movement allotted to the beat, the players look for indications of tonal character, dynamic level or levels (crescendo, diminuendo, forte, piano, etc.), emotional intensity, length, relation to the phrase, its value relative to the first beat of the succeeding measure, whether it is part of a leading harmonic progression or cadencial movement, and other factors created by acoustics and balance. How he combines all of these elements will variously affect the "personality" or quality of the beat, but this must not be allowed to change its unmistakable identity. If a composer should picture a new and different nature for the first beat of each measure, the conductor is obliged to relay that fact *within* its vertical attitude downward motion. Similarly, the other beats must be conceived and communicated within their own identity. Character, as well as identity, is thus necessary for meaningful utterance, and the conductor can find both in the score.

This does not mean that there is no merit in the prevailing method of learning the more or less standard directional movements—for the divisions of one, two, three, four, five, six, seven, eight, nine or twelve beats to a measure—and applying them wherever the time signature calls for them. But, as in most "systems" of learning, there are advantages and disadvantages.

With pedantic training, under competent direction, almost anyone may become adept, accurate and even fluent in the execution of the required beat patterns. One might, conceivably, reach the stage where, at the mere mention of a number, the arms would immediately and automatically describe the appropriate figure. Excellent! Now, let us apply this "technique" to a score. The signature is 3/4. We ascertain what we believe to be the tempo, and off we go without any problem. The hands know exactly what to do in order to indicate three to a measure. Then we take another score, this time in 3/8. Again, no problem. Repeat the procedure as to tempo, and rely confidently on our skill to beat three to a measure.

But wait! what about all the ingredients that make up the musical character of each beat, not to speak of each note? Will they all fit into the precast forms or containers into which we must now stuff the extra instructions we are committed to convey, in addition to the time and place of the beat? Are the acquired motions of habit flexible enough to expand and contract continually as the temperature of beat and phrase changes? Rarely. And what about the different kinds of tri-time? Are 3/4, 3/8, 3/16 the same? Does the "beat habit" take into account the difference between them? Or between 4/4, 4/2 and 4/8? Aren't we, by this limited method, risking the predicament of our friend in an earlier chapter who said to his orchestra, "This is the only way I was taught to beat five to a measure and you will just have to get it from my beat."?

In theory, the "method" sounds plausible. However, in application, it disregards the positive relationship of the substance to the source, somewhat like trying to create branches and leaves apart from their roots and trunk, putting them together as the occasion demands. Such branches, however expertly designed, will be artificial even when attached to a live tree. So will the separately developed beat patterns appear when applied to the music. To appear natural and express the character of a tree, the branches and leaves must grow out of the living trunk. Similarly, the substance (physical technique) must grow out of the living essence of the music which is enshrined in the source (the score). The motions within the technique should undoubtedly constitute a reflex action, but they should be a reflection of our total understanding, not an automatic, mechanical procedure.

8 | *Psychology in conducting*

Great men in the art of conducting are distinguished by their ability to fuse the source, substance and sound into a single entity of communication between composer and audience. To them, the study, preparation, physical development, authority, power, and even prestige are but the crude ores, metals and minerals which must be mixed and forged into the proper alloy. Glory, financial success, adulation and privilege are not the ends toward which they strive, but the means to continue in their devotion to the art.

In order to blend two or more ingredients correctly, it is necessary to be thoroughly familiar with the nature of each one, its strength and weakness, the possible reaction of one to the other, and be able to anticipate the character of the resulting mixture in its eventual state. The conductor, fusing the minds of composer, player and listener, must know the chemistry of human behavior, at least as it affects his working relationships.

However, the study of "psychology in conducting" has been somewhat overshadowed by the emphasis placed on learning to conduct by conducting, with little or no time devoted to the ways and means of preparing for the personal cooperation so vital to ensemble performance. We speak of a "rapport" between all concerned, but do little to explain how it can be achieved. It is not enough to say, "Be nice to the orchestra and they will play for you." At best, the orchestra will not resent a conductor who behaves in a gentlemanly fashion, but this is not the kind of "rapport" either desires. Courtesy, in itself, is merely a matter of good taste in human relationship of any kind. The orchestra wants and will contribute eagerly to a "rapport" established on the basis of musical integrity and mutual respect as performing partners. No conductor can receive or command respect by predecision or specific action. Every fibre of his body, every gesture, every glance must be motivated by a genuine understanding of the players as people and as accomplished musicians. The requirements for an interweaving of thought and emotion are as numberless as the notes, as changeable as each moment, and as fleeting as each sound, *hardly to be dismissed as a secondary facet of study.*

The dictionary defines "psychology" as, *"that branch of metaphysics which has for its subject the human soul, its nature, properties and operations; the sum of knowledge concerning the mind and mental operations."* It could also be defined as the science of human action and reaction.

Why is this knowledge so important to the conductor? Supposedly, he works with a product (score) created by a craftsman (the composer) in a recognizable form. His object is to translate that product into combinations of known sounds and values, employing instruments of specific nature as indicated. No psychological problems seem to be involved. Yet, if any one element of the conductor's equipment could be considered more important than the others, it might well be the "psychological factor." For, as we conceive it, it takes into its scope the manner in which the conductor places himself at the disposal of the composer, the manner by which he relates what he finds in the score to every player under his command, and the way in which this is then communicated to the audience in a genuine aesthetic experience.

| ···· |

Let us explore this process in two sections. We will examine first, the conductor's reaction to the action of the composer.

A musical composition is a recording of an emotional utterance, a visual rendering of thoughts and feelings. Expression of thought and feeling is the result of many related forces; learning, environment, personal emotion or involvements, sociological implications, habits, and dreams to which all of these contribute. The conductor cannot justifiably try to rationalize away, in favor of his own notions, the influence of background, training or indoctrination inherent in a composer's work. Because of this, the conscious intellectual presentation and development cannot be divorced from the subconscious. Everything the composer tries to say is in some way affected by what he has heard, seen or believes. In fact, the sum of his subconsious impulses constitutes the very soul of his conscious utterance.

The common system of notation, circumscribed as it is, in contrast with the intangible nature of sound itself makes it almost impossible for a composer to completely expose his inner being on paper, even if he should consciously wish to do so. For this reason, the performer or re-creator is constantly being exhorted to search for the hidden meaning in the music, to seek beneath and between and beyond the notes, in an effort to find the ephemeral "essence" of the composer's intentions.

Among those so charged is, of course, the conductor. He must identify himself even more closely with the composer than others, because of the danger that some details may be lost in the reflection by the orchestra. In seeking such identification, the score is only a starting point. It contains all the words with the proper grammar and necessary punctuation, but, as with the spoken word, the inspiration and motivation govern the degree of inflection which may change the meaning or force of a phrase, thereby affecting the sense of the whole.

The conductor should, by every possible means, familiarize himself with the composer as a human being, try to find the minutest details of his life—from infancy, if possible—his heritage, home life, love-life, social and political opinions, teachers, friends, problems, successes and failures, hopes, mode of dress, habits. He will be aided by knowledge of the social, political and cultural climate of the era in which the composer lived, with particular attention to events which might have, however remotely, influenced him at various periods in his life.

With this comprehensive information, the conductor prepares a mental picture of the composer and his environs into which he can project himself, submerge his own psyche in that of the composer, and, in effect, become his alter ego.

The utilization of psychology *in* conducting, therefore, encompasses a capability for thought transference —backward, through the subjection of one's own ego to that of the composer, and forward, through the influence brought to bear on orchestra and audience.

This dual process—submission to the composer and simultaneous command over all of the elements in performance—produces strange distortions when not properly understood. It is primarily failure in this respect which has produced a harmful confusion between what can be called the myth of a "conductor personality" and the actual "personality of the conductor."

Among impatient students, for example, and poorly prepared conductors, it has become almost a fetish to adopt deliberately what they believe to be, a "conductor personality." In the process, a strange and sudden metamorphosis occurs when many musicians step up on the podium. They move differently, speak differently, appear to think differently, and disport themselves in so unusual a manner that one is hard put to recognize the person who, a moment before, had been an interested listener or a participating player. If this occurs with a conductor who has not played in orchestras, it is considered an unfortunate circumstance. But when it also happens to musicians who have been orchestral players for years, it becomes a baffling phenomenon.

Over and over again, the same questions are asked. How can a normally quiet, dedicated, considerate and competent individual turn himself into a brash conceited tyrant merely by changing positions? Why do so many feel this personality change is necessary? What do they hope to achieve by this?

None of these questions is easy to answer, because they are intertwined and developed within the mental operations of each person affected. If we should want to justify this psychological aberration, we might accept certain mitigating factors. Perhaps a latent desire to exert more influence over the music than was possible as a player comes to the fore. Perhaps the new perspective, with its vastly expanded horizons, has a strange and powerfully exhilarating effect. Standing on the podium can be like standing on the highest mountaintop with all the world—past, present and future—laid out to be molded and affected by the movement of a hand or the nod of a head. The enormity of this challenge can drain all the rational power from the brain, as does the rarefied air of extremely high altitude, unless one is intellectually and carefully acclimated. Perhaps it is the release of all the pent up inhibitions imposed by other conductors, together with an outright inherent resentment to authority other than their own that accounts for a volatile attitude. Perhaps it is the strange sensation—akin to drunkenness—of looking out at the orchestra as from the small end of a funnel, causing the new world of the conductor to appear in peculiar perspective.

Any one or all of these could be contributory factors, but they would be reasons after the fact. We have to look into the motivation, behind the deliberate intent to change, in order to find out "why."

The prime cause is the kind of ignorance which allows potential conductors (and audiences) to accept as fact, inaccurate or exaggerated reports describing the behavior of certain famous conductors. It may also be induced by a naïveté which prompts them to believe, without doubt or personal research, what they are told. Anecdotes concerning the more explosive actions of conductors have been repeated so often, exaggerated and enhanced in the process, that they have become examples of "tradition." (Tradition is a handy little catchword that grants legitimacy and authority to exaggeration, distortion and sometimes deliberate disregard of a composer's written intentions.)

In a society which holds tradition more sacred than logic, there is a widespread belief that to be a great conductor one must be a combination of oracle, dictator, slave-driver and irrational, self-centered, egomaniac. This is the common image of the "conductor personality." The average person, musician and layman alike, is all too willing to believe in this exciting and romantic kind of personality, and blindly defends his concept of the conductor as a different species of being. Since "tradition" establishes these characteristics as evidence of greatness, ipso facto, this "conductor personality" must be assumed when one steps on the podium. That is why many conductors fall into the trap of "personality change," most of them achieving nothing more than an incongruous attitude and the silent ridicule of their orchestras.

A look behind the famous anecdote told of Toscanini may illustrate how the misunderstanding of a personality can develop. The incident is one that occurred during a rehearsal when Toscanini smashed his highly prized gold watch which had been presented to him by the members of the orchestra. No sooner had the story leaked through the doors of the rehearsal hall, when it was reported that, "The old man" had smashed his watch in a fit of temper because the orchestra did not give him what he wanted. Most of those who heard this report pounced on it with great glee and no questions. They passed it on from one to another with the affection afforded a bit of juicy gossip. Few cared to know what really led up to it, for this was in the accepted tradition of behavior expected of a great conductor. It was another manifestation of his genius to those who liked Toscanini, and an example of his inadequacy to those—thankfully in the minority—who were less than completely enthusiastic about him. Here was one of the rare momentary happenings that go into the making of a legend.

Everyone knows the story, but how many know the truth, or want to? How many are aware of the long, tiring hours of preparation, the mental and physical energy Toscanini poured into the effort to achieve his conviction of the score, the numerous quietly controlled attempts to draw his musical conception from the orchestra, and finally, the intense anguish which caused him to destroy something he valued dearly?

No—the outburst wasn't in anger at the orchestra at all!

It was an explosion brought on by overwhelming frustration within himself due to a seeming inability to create an image in accordance with his own uncompromising standards.

The prosaic day-to-day study and work, the problems, disappointments, restrictions and demands are the inner parts of the entity "conductor"; similar to the bones, muscles and heart which give shape and direction to a living being. But these areas under the skin are not glamorous, and must be kept hidden lest some sensitivities be offended. Only the outside face and figure are displayed to their most endearing and best advantage, and in the thrill of this display, there is a tendency to forget what lies beneath the surface.

The layman can be excused for ignoring the anatomy and gazing only upon the surface aspects of the art, but students and conductors must not be lulled, by precedent or tradition, into viewing their art in the same shallow way. The so-called "conductor personality" is not real. It is a figment of imagination made up of tiny scraps of half-truths and misunderstood actions such as I have illustrated.

In their need for living idols upon whom to lavish their admiration and affection, audiences have placed the conductor on a pedestal as a symbol representing all those involved in an orchestral performance. As a result, conductors who seek self-gratification through the apparent power afforded the "maestro"—and they are many—fancy themselves among the gods on Olympus, regarding the composition as the light in which they shine, and the orchestra as a vehicle for their aggrandizement. This is the psychological orientation of the "conductor personality" so eagerly assumed.

The "personality of a conductor" is quite another thing. It is the ultimate identifying feature of each individual, and cannot be taken up or put off at will, any more than one can remove or replace one's head. As the conductor's most formidable asset, it is the psychological bridge between himself and the orchestra, the route over which knowledge and conscience can travel both ways.

Like a radar screen, the "personality" must be attuned to sense the thoughts of the players as indicated by their actions. A conductor who is highly sensitive appears to have extra-sensory perception as he anticipates and counteracts every action during the playing of a complicated score. Astounding as it seems, this skill, or feat of personality, is one that can be developed as part of the technique of conducting. Although it falls in the realm of psychology because it is a mental process, the act of selecting and matching known facts continuously, at a rate of speed faster than sound, is nevertheless a technical procedure.

| ···· |

This brings us to the second section: the conductor's action and his reactions to the conscious and subconscious actions of the orchestra.

Before the conductor approaches the proximity of his players for rehearsal or performance, he has, presumably, established his relationship with the composer, conceived every detail of his musical projection, and laid plans for the accomplishment of it according to his knowledge of the abilities of the players he is to conduct.

Like a baseball manager, he will have "scouted" the orchestra personally, or through a trusted representative. The moment he comes into the rehearsal area, his personal radar should go into action. He needs to sense the attitude of the players toward him, toward music, toward their job. He must look for the signs that indicate the mood of each player; nervousness, dejection, exhilaration, fear, over-confidence, egotism, etc. The conductor's interest and concern should go much further, if at all possible. Personal problems, financial situation and physical health affect, in large measure, the players' contribution, and must be reckoned with.

All of these considerations, and more, are quite properly within the technique of conducting, since it is the reaction to this information that determines the conductor's approach to his orchestra at any given time. Understanding the player, as a human being, helps the conductor set a pace, know when and where he may force, with whom he should relax, and, most important, what references to use in order to make himself understood clearly, quickly and without arousing animosity.

Many conductors tend to forget they are charged to convey to the orchestra, in a split second, everything they themselves learned about the music through months, or perhaps years, of study and research. The task is a herculean one, and requires deep insight, and sympathy for the orchestra as people for its best accomplishment.

As for the orchestra, its over-all conception of the conductor could almost sum up the entire subject. They generally look upon their conductor with a strange kind of affection. To them, he is father, teacher, witch doctor, lawyer, philosopher, medicine man, dictator, politician, salesman, confessor and friend, all in one. And in all of these qualities they have faith, a faith which, if once broken by a conductor, is most difficult to renew. But by maintaining the faith, orchestra and conductor can achieve the ideal relationship—the state of "good rapport."

A great many conductors would be highly incensed if they were to be accused of "not keeping the faith." They would protest vigorously, and proclaim their love for music and regard for the orchestra without any compunction, never thinking that their actions could belie their words. Most seem unaware of two facts: first, players respond primarily to the conductor's motions, not to his words; and second, everything said at rehearsal is valid only to the extent to which the same instructions are given in motion. Verbal instructions, during rehearsal, cannot override or be considered a substitute for the physical direction at the concert. Even if they would wish to accept such a substitute, the natural tendency of players to react to what they see would cause confusion and indecision.

Every performance is a creation of the moment, not to be confused with imitation or repetition of something achieved at rehearsal. At a performance, the psychological factors are unique; the air becomes vibrant with anticipation, attention is sharply focused on the music to the exclusion of all else, and each member of the orchestra relinquishes his individuality while subjecting his mind and body to the conductor. All personal dreams and problems are postponed, to allow every nerve and fiber of the body to receive and act on the conductor's communication. This is another distinct psychological phenomenon.

Great conductors acknowledge it for what it is, and use it deliberately with confidence. They recognize it as the result of hope, pride, ambition, anxiety, devotion and determination on the part of the players, stimulated by the presence of the audience, the listeners, who alone can make the utterance complete.

Lesser conductors, who are mostly trained mechanics with conceit, feel it is *they* who have inspired it. By exposing this belief, they reveal their ignorance of psychology as part of the conducting technique, and go on to commit many of the acts that add up to "breaking the faith."

One of these offenses is the lack of ability to use rehearsal time intelligently. During years spent observing the procedure of conductors, from rehearsal through performance, I have found a surprisingly large number who do not seem to know the real reason for rehearsal. Some use it as a means of learning the score by hearing it played. Some use it as a practice period for themselves, with little concern for the orchestra. Some use up the time talking, in a fear-inspired attempt to impress the orchestra with their musical erudition. And some pour all their energy, knowledge and power into frantic attempts to reach a performance peak (artificial at best), leaving the orchestra and themselves tired and emotionally drained.

The conductors who take advantage of the orchestra at rehearsal, in order to learn their craft or bolster their ego, are obviously incompetent and inconsiderate. Those who strive so desperately for a performance level show their apprehension and fundamental insecurity. They are, most frequently, well-prepared but, at performance, become nervous or inhibited. This is why they struggle to achieve musical satisfaction where, they mistakenly believe, they are not being judged.

But what is rehearsal for?

To put it simply, the purpose of rehearsal is to *prepare for performance*. It cannot be anything else. A rehearsal is a period of time in which the player (not the conductor) should have the opportunity to play the music and solve any of its technical problems, learn how the conductor speaks for the composer, and adjust bowing, fingering and phrasing accordingly. It is a time for the conductor to present his understanding of the score and help the players accomplish it, to stop, repeat and explain as he finds it necessary, to make everything ready for the moment when the audience will lend its subjection to complete the chain begun by the composer.

The expectancy and receptivity of an audience provide the all-important spark needed to light the fire in which the separate elements are fused. Without this fire and the unbroken continuity of performance, the soul of the music remains no more than a promise.

As a result of proper mental preparation to face the orchestra, the conductor cannot fail to realize now that whatever he does is related to and determined by its needs. Every movement must have a purpose and a meaning. His hands must be clear and visible to everyone, or they serve no useful purpose. His total attention must be directed toward the orchestra every moment, or he loses contact and control. He must change *his* own motions in order to compensate for discrepancies in ensemble or problems of sound production, look for inattention and counteract it, lend confidence, by a glance, to players who may be fearful or nervous before a difficult passage, assure all, by his complete interest in them, they need not worry about an entrance as he will be there to guide them, and generally, give the impression that he is deeply involved with every part all of the time. In the process of doing this with sincerity and skill, it will quickly become evident that he is "making music" together with the orchestra, the final realization of his function.

The act of intimate mental association with each player is the forward transference mentioned earlier. The composite psyche, a blend of composer and conductor, is now superimposed upon the mind of each

109 | Psychology in conducting

player individually, and the orchestra collectively; causing them to become as one, and achieving the ultimate in communication.

| •••• |

Every conductor, who has had sufficient association with his media plus an enlightened attitude, knows that mistakes may be made in performance despite the best intentions and rehearsal efforts; by *him* as well as the players. As part of his background, he learns where they are most likely to occur, and prepares to cope with them, overcome them or minimize the results. The skill with which he manages this reveals the extent of his maturity.

When a player makes a mistake in performance, he is always immediately aware of it. He feels shame, embarrassment, hurt pride, and is genuinely remorseful. Since a wrong sound is irrevocable, it serves no purpose for the conductor to grimace, react with a gesture, or otherwise call attention to the mistake at that moment. He must, instantaneously, try to determine the possible cause of the error and make a decision relative to that cause. If the contributing factors are mechanical, or in any way beyond his actual control, he should file the incident away in his mind for later analysis and correction. But, should there be the slightest possibility that the mistake was caused, even in part, by a misunderstanding of his communication to the orchestra, he is obliged to make every effort to avoid a repetition of this contributing factor.

With all this to do in the split second during which a mistake occurs, is there time to make a wry face or gesture of disdain? And what happens to the music while this is going on? Even if the conductor's reaction is momentary, some part of a phrase will not receive his full concentration. Without realizing it and certainly without intent, he can, in this way, compound the damage done by a mistake, whether or not he had any responsibility for its cause.

There are, of course, various reasons why a conductor reacts as he does. The most easily condoned reason is the hypersensitivity of one who is completely immersed in his concept of the score. Any deviation will affect him with an almost physical force, causing him to wince as from an unexpected blow. Such sincere reaction usually evokes sympathy from the orchestra, out of their common dedication, and the conductor who senses this will not digress in performance to chastise a player or vindicate himself.

Many conductors feel it is necessary to exaggerate their reaction to every error in order to prove they are astute, know the score thoroughly and hear everything. Quite often, we find one who thinks it necessary to let the players know "they cannot fool him," or "get away with anything." It is particularly interesting, for, almost without exception, no orchestral player really tries to "fool" the conductor or "get away with anything." His own pride and training assure his best efforts. Also, it is very rare that the orchestra does not hear and recognize a mistake at the same time. In fact, they know the cause before the conductor becomes aware of it. What, then, is accomplished when a conductor directs at a player what is called "a dirty look," or claps his hand to his head in despair, or pulls one ear lobe? Even, as I have seen at one performance, pretend to stab himself with the baton!

Whatever the gesture, the results are never satisfactory. The concentration is disturbed, the musical line is broken, and conditions for a build-up of hostility are established. The more such reactions, the greater the potential danger of mistakes, leading to more actual mistakes which might otherwise not be made. Such a situation has been described by players as, "being expected to play flawlessly while walking on raw eggs, with loss of your career and reputation as the penalty for breaking one."

Happily, there is common ground on which everyone concerned can meet, and from which each one starts. It lies in an earnest desire for the best possible performance, shared by conductor, orchestra and audience. In the coordinated effort to achieve this universal objective, the orchestra, too, has an obligation in the establishment of the "good rapport," as does the audience to a lesser degree. *It is the conductor, however, who must carry the lion's share of personal mental discipline.*

His consideration of "psychology in conducting" cannot be limited to his relationships with composer and orchestra. Just as he can influence the contribution of his players, he is also in a position to direct the attitude of the audience. Planning for the effect his movements will have upon the audience is also part of "psychology in conducting," and deserves more attention than it normally receives. Every audience has its own personality. The atmosphere developed as a "Saturday night" audience assembles, for example, is markedly different from the mood displayed on Friday afternoon, or any other time. The experienced stage performer is intensely aware of this, as it calls for a change of pace and timing in order to avoid losing contact with the listener. Conductors have the same problem to contend with. The attention of the audience must be gained, channelled, and held so that the communication can be completed.

The conductor should be alert to the atmosphere generated by the audience in the auditorium, even before he steps upon the stage. If it is gay, with a high noise level and the excitement of much chattering, he must compensate for it on his way to the podium. When an audience is subdued, and the opening music calls for a feeling of gaiety, he must lead to this mood with his physical attitude. The tempo of his walk to the podium, the weight of his steps, the angle of his head, are some of the means with which he can adjust the attention of the audience to his suggestion. He should aim to take his listeners from their tempo and mood to the color and character of the opening measures of the music, with predecision, as he would lead the orchestra itself through a retard or accelerando to a new section.

Once he begins to conduct, his own devotion to the music determines the concentration level of his audience. If the conductor calls undue attention to himself, by his behavior on the podium, interest in the music will diminish. The audience will be quickly divided into two groups in reaction to disturbing movements of his arms and body, those who are entertained and those who are annoyed. Whatever the ratio between these groups may be, everyone will be distracted from the original purpose of the performance. With the focus thus shifted from audial to visual, from sound to sight, the quality of performance is jeopardized, the composer is relegated to a secondary position, and the orchestra becomes a setting for the display of the conductor. This adds up to a complete negation of all the reasons for the existence of the contemporary conductor.

| .... |

There can be no concessions in the acceptance of the

conductor's function or in the application thereof, despite theory and tradition. If further proof is needed, the following facts will serve:

One:

The composer can create without the presence of a conductor.

Two:

The orchestra can play a fair amount of music without a conductor.

Three:

The conductor, without composition or orchestra, can ....?

9 | *Function and responsibility in the light of experience*

The function and responsibility of the modern conductor is a subject so vast it defies academic description. There are no boundaries or limitations within which it can be confined. Each new composition enlarges its area; each new listener adds to its scope; each new performance increases its importance. Any restriction of fulfillment is created only by the conductor himself, in proportion to his understanding and vision.

This section has been compiled to extend the horizon of the reader beyond the theory and logic of analysis. Theory can be challenged, and rationalization may often be mistaken for logic if one does not look for proof and validation. In the final evaluation, our conclusions must be checked against the results gained through experience. Not the experience of a few persons who may be known to us as exemplary figures in one or another phase of performance, but the musical, academic, physical and human experiences of as many as possible, regardless of the area in which they utilize their abilities.

It is a serious fallacy to assume that the experience and opinions of a conductor who is predominantly engaged with film music or the musical theatre are not of prime value to one aspiring to conduct a symphony orchestra, or vice versa. A number of our most highly skilled conductors are engaged in creating and performing (not always by their own choice) what an uninformed society has labelled, "lesser music." Economics, generally, determines this situation despite any aesthetic ambitions.

Every conductor is concerned with the same source, substance and human elements, and, indeed, the divergence of their viewpoints provides the only realistic cross-check available, short of experiencing everything one's self. Since this is impossible, the best substitute is access to the thoughts of many authorities who have had wide experience.

Wisdom is acquired by seeking within ourselves and within the minds of others. And it is in this spirit the opinions of some of the most enlightened and potent minds of our time are presented—opinions of men whose collective activities encompass every facet of musical endeavor; education, symphony, opera, ballet, films and television. The varied background and tradition reflected in their statements provide a most fertile area of reference for all who want to understand the role of the modern conductor.

Each of the eminent authorities who have contributed to this chapter was asked, "What, in your opinion, is the primary function and responsibility of the conductor?"

LEOPOLD STOKOWSKI

Music Director of American Symphony Orchestra, Philadelphia Symphony, New York Philharmonic, NBC, All-American Youth Orchestra, guest conductor with every major orchestra throughout the world.

"The responsibility and complex task of the conductor is to convey from the composer to the listener the full message of the music. If the composer was in an inspired mood that inspiration must be in the playing of the orchestra. Orchestra and conductor are merely the means to a great end, which is the communication of feeling and beauty that is the privilege of listeners, when they are receiving the great musical ideas of masters such as Bach and Beethoven."

WILLIAM SCHUMAN

*President of the Lincoln Center for the Perform-
ing Arts; Distinguished composer; formerly
President of the Juilliard School of Music.*

". . . To me a conductor has two principal functions, the first societal (and by that I do not mean
the drawing room social) and the second musical.
By societal I mean the obligation of the conductor to function as a leader in his community. The
demands on this leadership vary, of course, with
particular communities, but the conductor must be
the leader, the teacher, the guide, the spiritual
head. If we remember always that music is human
communication through the medium of sound, it
follows then that the conductor's role is educational
(societal) because it is he who chooses and super-
vises the quality of the sounds which are communicated. This means, therefore, that no part of the
conductor's obligation is more important than the
choice of repertory. It is repertory, not performance, that is the basis of the art of music. Performance is, of course, the life channel of repertory.
Repertory in purest terms demands performers who
are able to reveal specific qualities through tech-

nical mastery and aesthetic insight. It is only these considerations which can constitute a true measure of evaluation for the skill of performers. While these considerations are, of course, professional and musical, they are basically societal because the prime issue is really moral.

The conductor's musical obligation toward the composer is to infuse the music with his own re-creative skills, which, in turn, imply the utmost in flexibility that can be achieved without distortion of the text. It is sometimes believed that a faithful adherence to the text does not give sufficient lee-way for "interpretation." While the hieroglyphics of a score can in themselves but suggest the emotional intention of the composer, they can reveal quite precisely his intellectual intention. It is false to assume, however, that the intellectual intention can be realized without the performer's emotional involvement. This composer, at least, hopes always for a performance which comes from inside the performer, which is of such sympathy that, while he is performing, he recreates the composer—in short, then, flights of fancy within the stated intention of the creator, controlled by the disciplines of high art."

JOSEF KRIPS

> *Conductor: San Francisco Symphony, New York Philharmonic, and guest conductor with every major symphony orchestra throughout the world.*

"There is, in reality, one single requirement for a conductor. Of course he must have a certain personality and the ability to convey his wishes to the orchestra. But most important of all is his musicianship. Each orchestra, good, mediocre or bad, will know after five minutes whether the conductor is a real musician or just a man who beats the time.

The so-called "technique of conducting" in itself can be taught and learned in a very short time, but the musicianship is something a conductor has to work on a whole lifetime. A conductor has to make his orchestra "sing" and not just play. The beauty of sound of an orchestra is the sum of the produced harmonics or overtones. Any kind of rough or dead playing (routine playing) makes it impossible to produce such harmonics.

To be a conductor is a twenty-four hour job, 365 days a year. Every day new music is created and the conductor has to read and to study the music he selects, and besides that, one has to re-study, even after forty years of a conducting career, all works on the program. The conductor has to feel as a member of the orchestra: a very impor-tant one. If he doesn't feel this way, he will not get the response of his musicians, because a real fine performance needs, besides the fingers and lips of the musicians, their complete heart and dedica-tion. Besides that, the conductor must be a fine psychologist, too, because he has to win at every rehearsal and every performance anew the trust and, if possible, the love of his musicians.

When an orchestral musician awakes in the morning, he is already offended because he knows he will be abused by the conductor, by the man-agement, by the press, just by anybody. So the con-ductor has to bring his musicians, at the very be-ginning of each rehearsal, into a dedicated mood to the music. Above all, a conductor has to realize that he is the servant of the composer whose works he performs. His work is very important, but should not appear so.

How many times, during his career, does a mu-sician have to rehearse Beethoven's Eroica Sym-phony, just as one example? And even if every con-ductor thinks he is just asking for what is in the score, each single reading and each single per-formance will be different. To follow even the de-mands of every good conductor means, for an or-chestra musician, not only a great ability on his instrument, but also a limitless dedication to his profession."

DR. HOWARD HANSON

Director of the Eastman School of Music, University of Rochester; Distinguished Conductor, composer and musicologist.

". . . A great deal has been written about conducting technic, scoring, baton technic, "communication," and the like. Obviously, all of these matters are important but whereas the first three elements are, I believe, capable of development by study, the matter of communication involves elements which must be innate and cannot be 'learned.'

Obviously, in order to communicate, one must have something to communicate. One of my best friends, one of the great conductors, was Serge Koussevitzky and I can remember his speaking again and again of "reading behind the notes." What he meant, obviously, was the ability of the conductor to see behind the notes into the mind of the composer, to try to ascertain the purpose for which the music was written and to become an interpreter of that purpose.

This power of communication seems to affect not only the interpretation of the musical score but the actual sound of the orchestra itself. I remember many years ago going with Serge Koussevitzky to a rehearsal of the New York Philharmonic with which he was appearing as a guest conductor. It was amazing to see that orchestra, within the matter of an hour, beginning to take on the color and the sound of the Boston Symphony in the Koussevitzky days. I think it is perfectly proper to speak of the Koussevitzky sound, the Stokowski sound, Ormandy, Szell, Leinsdorf, and so forth. In fact, every distinguished conductor who has this power to communicate seems to produce from the orchestra his own particular kind of sound.

We have all had the experience of seeing an orchestra under a great conductor play far above and beyond its own natural capability. This is, I believe, essentially a psychic rather than a musical phenomenon, although it must obviously depend on musical knowledge, sensitivity and inspiration. In certain instances, it could almost be likened to a form of hypnotism. This seems to me to be in the final analysis what distinguishes a great conductor from a competent one."

LEON BARZIN

Music Director of the Nationale Philharmonie de Paris; formerly Musical Director of the National Orchestral Association, New York City Ballet Company and Radio Station WQXR.

"I am tremendously impressed by the contents of this book with its focus on the function and responsibility of the contemporary conductor. My extensive experience as a Conductor and as a guide for others has confirmed my belief that one must first realize the nature of his position and what is expected of him before he can begin to prepare for the duties of a conductor.

It is important to understand, from the very beginning, that the man behind the baton must be ready to fulfill all the demands made by any position which may present itself. He must be capable of serving music in all its varied aspects—symphony, opera, musical comedy, radio, television, etc. Voluntary restriction to specific fields represents a limitation in ideas and ability.

The preparation of a conductor is the same for any form of presentation, and calls for, first, a profound knowledge of music in general plus the mastery of and experience with one or more orchestral instruments. Then, if an aptitude for leadership becomes apparent—in a first chair position or coaching capacity—the individual possessing such talent is ready to begin his development of the art of conducting.

This art, with its physical, mental and aesthetic requirements, is clarified within this book, but I should like to call attention to an area of preparation which is woefully lacking in today's society. The practise field which is so important in the training of our young (25 to 40 years of age) talents. In the past, conductors had the opportunity of using, as proving grounds, the silent movies—where hundreds of pieces had to be played each week, and where they had to adjust quickly to the picture—vaudeville, and operetta. This experience was not as far removed from contemporary ballet, symphony and opera as one might think. Today these fields are practically non-existent; on top of which, economic problems limit the time allowed for preparation of any performance, so the modern conductor must work twice as fast and have at least as much facility as any of our outstanding instrumental soloists.

However, all of this preparation and ability is in serious danger of being wasted because those who choose a conductor—Board of Directors, managers, etc.—are not sufficiently prepared for their responsibilities. Their preparation lies in learning to understand the true function and relationships of the score, the conductor and the orchestra, as

they understand the rules of baseball or appreciate
the timing of a fine tennis player.

To be ready for a major position, the conductor
must be prepared with a wide repertory with which
to stimulate the musical life of the community. To
insure such musical progress, every sincere music
lover, and particularly those in positions of authority, should do his or her best to select the right
conductor through knowledge and not through
personal instinct. In this way, performer and listener alike can help our country move forward in
the arts."

GEORGE BALANCHINE

Artistic Director and Choreographer of the New York City Ballet Company.

"In our experience in the New York City Ballet, a conductor must have a strong sense of rhythm, be completely true to the score and responsible for the exact execution of the composer's wishes. The conductor should have the ability to become physically involved with rhythmic pulsation pattern and have sufficiently trained reflexes to enable fulfillment of this function. Also it is exceedingly helpful to be familiar with the visual part of the dance.

Above all this, a musical sensitivity and taste is desirable and necessary to translate the composer's intentions from the printed page to the hearing ear and the dancing feet."

SKITCH HENDERSON

Musical Director, National Broadcasting Company, New York.

"The art of conducting has very little to do with music these days. If we are to believe the historians and what has gone before, the concert master used to assert his authority to try to keep the orchestra together. But this was long before any of the comprehensive teaching school, as we know it today.

The first conductors were the metronomes of the day, but little by little the folly of man has inserted itself. With only one or two exceptions, the conductor has become an invisible wall between the lay public and the orchestra. He has preened himself to look fashionable, to outdo the Barrymore family in curtain calls (in vaudeville we called it milking applause), to surround himself with the peculiar sophistication and glamour that has nothing whatsoever to do with the concert hall.

In my opinion, time/tempo is the determining factor of music. The notes on the printed page, the style of composition, the skill of orchestration, the period of music—all these are completely vulnerable to the likes and dislikes of the fickle listener. Time never changes and should not change.

The type of professional musician who occupies each and every chair in the modern top grade symphony has been schooled and has devoted his or her life to a faithful reproduction of the printed score page. After fifteen or twenty years of hard study and research, our sartorial friend of the masses makes his agile leap to the exalted square known as the podium and begins to tear asunder what has gone before.

Quite obviously, there are and have been devoted and skilled men in the maestro school. But the odds are about 20–1 that you will ever have a chance to see as well as hear them. I recall with great fondness a violinist in the NBC Symphony who, after a particularly harrowing rehearsal with one of our glamour boys, said: "Please give us the downbeat—and get lost!"

And I have a hunch he was right."

THOMAS SCHERMAN

Music Director, Little Orchestra Society, Concert Opera Assn.

"My feeling is that the primary function of a conductor is one of a *teacher*. He must introduce new music to the community in which he lives, as well as his own personal and unique approach to the great musical masterpieces of the past, and in so doing *teaches* his audiences and raises their level of appreciation—making them musically more aware. But besides this important task, he must also teach music to the *players* under his baton. This might seem arrogant in the light of the high degree of technical excellence and musicianship of the average instrumental musician today, especially in this country. Actually, there are very few conductors living who can approach in technique and instrumental finesse that of the players whom they lead.

What today's conductor must teach the musicians, I feel, is fourfold.

In a piece of music they *already know*, he must teach them his *own* interpretation. Whether this interpretation, in the light of musical history and abstract esthetics, is good or bad, it is, nonetheless, definitely valid. Otherwise he would not be where he is, as one of the cultural leaders of the community. And the players can *learn* from this interpretation. It might seem too fast to some of them, or overly free rhythmically to others, but they can only learn something from it. For example, I vividly recall speaking to some of the musicians of a major symphony orchestra who had just been through a rehearsal under the baton of a guest conductor whom they despised (for *non*-musical reasons), and whom they were even prepared to boycott musically. After the first quarter hour of the rehearsal, they were responding to his every musical wish because he had something *important* to say musically, and to them it was new, valid, and exciting.

In a piece of music *new* to the players, the conductor must gradually get them sufficiently familiar with it, during the rehearsals so that they can anticipate when a passage they have to play is of primary importance in relation to the whole piece, or it is merely an accompaniment or still otherwise, when it falls within that difficult "in between" category. This, of course, is hard considering the limited rehearsal time available to most orchestras to prepare even the most difficult program. Therefore, the conductor must himself know the score so well that he can anticipate the difficult passages for each instrument or group of instruments, and help them out by being "right with them;" by his eyes, more than by his gestures, he can give them what amounts to be a pre-game pep-talk.

The teaching of the relative importance and the relative difficulty of each individual part leads a conductor to his third and, I feel, one of his most important functions as a teacher to the musicians. He must teach them to *listen* to each other. An orchestra is made up of as many musical personalities as there are players in it. However, they must play as one. A conductor must often do this hard task, not in three months, but in three *hours*. He can do it by pointing out to the first violin section, for example, that although they are playing what seems to be the dominant melody, they are being doubled, perhaps, by the flute or the oboe; and the flutist or oboist, being a soloist, is bound to have his own individual style of phrasing, and it is important that the violinists match *their* phrasing with that of the wind soloist. They can only do this by listening and it is up to the conductor to point out to them *what* to listen *for*.

Frequently, the conductor himself must adjust his musical thoughts to one or another of his players. For instance, his bassoonist may be a brilliant musician and technician, but incapable by temperament of playing a certain passage as slowly or as rapidly, as loudly or softly as the conductor would ideally wish. But rather than ruthlessly impose his musical will on the player, thereby risking a compromise or an unconvincing performance, the conductor should take advantage of the *plus* factors in the player's makeup and allow him during that particular passage to "have his head" and to be the temporary leader of the ensemble. But this should at all times be *guided* by the conductor and should always be *within the framework* of his interpretation as a whole. This fascinating give and take among the musicians and between the musicians and conductor form some of the most exciting experiences in music-making.

The fourth and probably most important teaching function of the conductor, to my mind, is that of style. It is commonplace today to say that a Mozart Symphony must be approached by the player in an entirely different manner than a D'Indy tone-poem, but unfortunately, too often even our best instrumentalists overlook this. Usually, they are instinctively "correct" in their approach, but when they are not, the conductor must tell them so and, if necessary, even tell them *why*. Often they may resent it, thinking their own approach is more valid, so the conductor must be 300% sure of his ground.

But when all is said and done, the fascinating thing is that besides being a teacher of the players, a conductor can and should *learn* from them at the same time. And it is this fact that makes conducting the most enriching and stimulating of all musical professions."

MAX RUDOLF

*Music Director of the Cincinnati Symphony;
formerly conductor and artistic administrator of
the Metropolitan Opera Company in New York.*

"The question of the "why" of conducting is based
on the assumption that an orchestra renders a better performance if led by a conductor and must be
answered on three levels: *technical, musical,* and
inspirational.

1. The *technical* aspect of the conductor's craft
points to a co-ordinating and time-saving activity.
The application of certain symbolic signs requires
knowledge and physical skill in order to assure perfect relationship between gesture and response. To
make the best use of rehearsals the conductor must
be a capable organizer of time. Wanting in these
technical skills he would complicate coordination
instead of facilitating it, and waste time instead of
utilizing it fully for quick results.

2. The conductor's *musical* task demands learning and perception how to interpret music, and
ability in advising musical performers. Insight into
all the elements of composition and familiarity with
musical styles enable the conductor to gain a con-

ception of the full score aiming to come as close as possible to the composer's intentions. Thus the conductor assumes the responsibility to serve as an intermediary between composer and players. Knowledge of all devices used by instrumental and vocal performers provides the competence needed to instruct his group and to realize his conception of the score.

3. The axiom that the recreation of music goes beyond the sum total of technical and musical details calls for *inspirational* qualities on the part of the conductor who is conscious of the teamwork on which the results of his endeavors depend. He must express his ideas and feelings with conviction to evoke enthusiasm in his co-workers. He must possess the intangible ability to convey the spirit of the music and to bring out the highest potential in the musicians he leads."

JOHN GREEN

Composer, Conductor, Arranger and Pianist. Music Director and Conductor of the Promenade concerts, Los Angeles Philharmonic Symphony Orchestra. Academy Award Winner. Active in the musical theatre, films and television as, "Johnny Green."

"The conductor's two prime functions are:

a) So to communicate with his orchestra as to provide the players with an instantaneous understanding of what he wishes them to do with the music. He must infuse the orchestra with either a whole-hearted willingness to do his bidding or with an inability to resist it.

b) Through the effectiveness of his orchestral command, his knowledge of and feeling for the work, and through the physical attractiveness (not necessarily graceful in a choreographic sense) of what he does with his hands, arms, head and body (as seen primarily from his back or, at most, in profile) to compel the audience's attention and sense of satisfaction. Therefore, the conductor's total effectiveness evolves from his capability in the following areas:

a) To bend instantly to his will the total abilities, techniques and talents of the players under his baton. It is "nicer" for both conductor and players if this is achieved in an atmosphere of affection and gemütlichkeit, but such an atmosphere is not de rigeur. In other words, a genuine talent for *leadership* is a sine qua non.

b) The ability to read an orchestral score fluently and to derive from such reading a full understanding of the form, line and logic of a composition, in addition to an *intimate* knowledge of its sheer notes, rhythms, meters and colors.

c) Having accomplished Item b, to be able instantly to communicate with the orchestra by means of a totally effortless and spontaneously functioning technique of arm, hand and stick movement, facial expression and body *management*. And by such communication to achieve an instant understanding from the orchestra of the conductor's interpretation of the work, such interpretation resulting from his achievement of the objectives in Item b. Clarity of beat, total avoidance of waste motion in arms, hands, body, face, head and eyes, crystal clear definition of bar lines, meter and important accent and uncomplicated indications of dynamics constitute the sine qua non here.

d) By achieving B and C, to give to the audience a sense of repose and a confidence that the conductor and orchestra share the same objectives, speak the same language and are fully "tuned in," each to the other.

A vital and indispensable factor in achieving all of the above is a specific and maximum coordination between the conductor's mind and his physical movement. This is as important to a conductor as it is to a champion athlete. The conductor's ability to translate thought, feeling and emotion into properly representational physical movement instantly and automatically, on a reflex basis without the necessity of one iota of conscious thought for the physical movement itself, is utterly essential for the effective conductor. This ideal coordination requires a gift to start with. Once it is established that the gift is there, it must then be developed through proper instruction and intensive and endless practise, again in the manner of the student athlete with championship ambitions.

The *ultimate* function of the conductor is to be the catalyst in bringing the fullest possible realization of the *intent* of the composer to the total "receiving apparatus" of the audience.

The "receiving apparatus" of the audience includes:

a) Its ears.
b) Its eyes (when in-person performance is involved whether it be live performance, on-screen TV or theatrical screen).
c) Its emotional "reactors" and nervous systems.
d) Its intellectual or conscious cerebral equipment."

SIDNEY HARTH

Chairman of the Music Department at Carnegie Institute of Technology; Violinist and Conductor.

"If there be any *primary* functions for a working conductor whatsoever, surely these functions must transcend the mere technical or musical or perhaps even the personal involvement of the musician himself. Taking for granted his skill, adeptness, basic sound concepts of the music, knowledge of the score, and of the orchestra as a performing body (I dislike the word 'instrument' in reference to an orchestra), assuming his experience, intelligent rehearsal procedure, diplomatic relationships with his men—and with his board of trustees!—what more, then, can one ask of the modern conductor?

I think this answer must be categorized into three sections:

1. *Musical functions:* From my experience, which includes solo playing, conducting, educational administration, teaching and not a few years as concertmaster of orchestras, the keynote is *projection*. This element—one which cannot be taught,

I fear,—is immediately clear to audience and orchestra and that conductor who can and will project to player and listener, no matter what his technical accomplishments or clarity may be, is performing his musical function.

2. *Educational function:* The art of programming is a difficult and far reaching influence. That
conductor who can continually educate his audience into better listening, selective listening, alert
listening, and tolerant understanding—and this can
take years—will be performing his musical function.

3. *Community function:* This is the sole category wherein the visiting or guest conductor has
no role to play; but it is important enough cul-
turally to certainly include in the necessary influences. An earnest serious conductor who wishes to
mold and build his ensemble to its utmost potential must be leader to his men and to the musical
community, offer himself as model to young and
old, be the paragon of musical virtue whether he
be concerned in the matters withdrawn from his
own immediacy, and in general be the dynamic
motivating musical force for the community in
which he resides."

STANISLAW SKROWACZEWSKI

Music Director, Minneapolis Symphony Orchestra.

"I would think that there are two primary functions of a conductor, both extremely important and both, of course, working parallel and simultaneously. The first lies in the conductor's knowledge of the STYLE. He must know and feel the peculiarities of each composer and even each work, and his interpretation must be subordinate to these peculiarities to the smallest detail. (The so highly estimated clearness of orchestra sounding has its value only if it shows the clearness of the style.)

The second primary function and responsibility of a conductor lies in the possibilities of adequate communication of his knowledge to the orchestra and full success in convincing and teaching all musicians how to do it. Thus I repeat after Franz Liszt—"the real task of a conductor consists in making himself almost useless." The question how to proceed with the orchestra, how to conduct (what kind of technique), how to rehearse, is absolutely already unimportant as far as some "prescription" could be proposed and belongs already to the secondary functions of a conductor's work as they depend on many other contributing outside factors."

IZLER SOLOMON

Music Director and Conductor, Indianapolis Symphony Orchestra.

"The primary function and responsibility of a Conductor is to communicate to his orchestra an interpretation of the music that has both integrity and recreative beauty.

To accomplish this the conductor must respect the composer's intent, and both Conductor and Orchestra must respect each other. This element of mutual respect develops as a result of various factors.

We assume that the Conductor has all of the necessary qualifications of musicianship, the ability to convey knowledge clearly and concisely, the ability to inspire his player and patience.

I personally believe it is necessary for the Conductor to show respect for his players and treat them as sensitive artists who actively create this great instrument—the Orchestra. He must also teach them that a great Orchestra has pride in itself.

Again assuming that the Conductor has the above musical qualifications—I believe this attitude on his part can and will bring respect from his players, which I feel is extremely important.

One can build a good Orchestra with deference, but a great Orchestra requires mutual respect."

HOWARD MITCHELL

Music Director, National Symphony Orchestra, Washington, D. C.

"I feel the primary functions and responsibility of a conductor are first, to exert forceful leadership over the music and the musicians in order to achieve the very best musical performance from a composition; and, second, to build and sustain interest in the orchestra in the entire community.

After making an intensive study of the composition to be performed, it is up to the conductor to use his technical skill to draw from the orchestra's multiple personalities its very best abilities. In an orchestra we are dealing with some 100 musicians, each one bringing his own personality to his own particular instrument. A certain strength of personality on the part of the conductor is necessary to maintain absolute musical authority, essential to any good performance.

The authority of a beat can be recognized and explained. But the authority of a personality with its infinite possibilities, both artistic and human, is still an enigma and probably will always remain so. The final net result of any performance is a combination of the conductor's innate skills, his artistic temperament and his human attributes.

Here in the United States conductors have a second responsibility. I refer now to those conductors of orchestras—more than 1,000—which are relatively new. These are the orchestras which have been born within the last 35 years and are still suffering growing pains. It is up to the conductors of these symphony orchestras to help form the musical tastes of the entire community, especially the young people. In this way the conductor will build and sustain interest in the resident orchestra.

More concerts for the young will not only be building live and interested audiences for the future, but will also reap benefits for today. They create good public relations with the parents of the children, with civic leaders, business, the schools—in short, the whole community. In the total symphony picture of today complete community support is an absolute must for an adequate budget, and an adequate budget is a must for artistic growth. This can only be accomplished by making the local symphony orchestra a vital force in the entire community—a living cultural asset."

HARWOOD SIMMONS

Professor of Music, School of Music, Syracuse University, Syracuse, New York.

"All heard music is a reproduction. The original disappears the moment it leaves the composer's mind to become a score. From then on its interpreters become masters of its fate and what any listener hears is at best like looking at a good, bad or indifferent reprint of a painting. The conductor-interpreter who displays this reprint to the listener accepts a great moral responsibility. Thus his primary function is to preserve and protect what he conceives to be the composer's original ideas. Any deviation from this purpose is highly questionable. The problem, therefore, is for the conductor to ascertain what the original ideas are, and to interpret them with every unit of talent, scholarship and technical facility at his command. The best conductor is the best musically and aesthetically educated conductor. Important secondary assets are diplomacy and personal magnetism.

Any conductor is, perforce, a kind of necessary evil in that he stands between the composer, the performers and the listener somewhat in the manner of a recording engineer who stands between the music as heard in the concert hall and the listener who hears only the reproduction.

Our conductor-interpreter faces his playing or singing interpreters as a go-between who must, of necessity, force his will upon artists whose own interpretations are to be respected but at the same time coordinated and often reshaped so that a cohesive, logical whole will result. Thus no conductor is able to convey completely his own feelings and ideas about the music at hand. Even the composer-conductor, in performing his own composition, must accept in part the interpretations of others and hope at best to impress most of his wishes upon them.

In sum, that intelligent and gifted musician with just the right amount of self-effacement combined with ample ability to communicate his interpretations, while guiding those of his co-interpreters, is fulfilling his function as a conductor."

JULIUS RUDEL

Director, New York City Opera Company.

"I consider the primary function of a conductor to be guide and leader of the musical ensemble with the responsibility of instilling in the performers an understanding of and feeling for the particular character of each composition, thereby producing a total performance with a true homogeneity of style."

ERNEST GOLD

Composer, Conductor, Academy Award Winner for film music. His compositions include symphonies, songs and music for television.

"I feel that the main function of a conductor is to convey to the orchestra the intent of the music and in doing so recreate the essence the composer had in mind. Moreover, it is his task to help his players accomplish that end by giving them indications of both technical and musical nature how to go about it.

Since the conductor cannot help but see the music through his own eyes, his manner of conducting will automatically reflect an interpretation that is his without any conscious effort in that direction."

ROBERT A. IRVING

Conductor, New York City Ballet.

"The functions of a conductor have lately become so inflated and distorted, that indeed the music and the musicians, who play it, seem to fill quite subsidiary roles. The glamour of some of these overpaid creatures attracts all manner of irresponsible people to this career, who seem to think that enthusiasm and physical attraction are sufficient. There is no doubt that a good conductor makes an immense difference, even to a first-rate orchestra, but it is perfectly simple to train any talented child to conduct the standard classics, if its parents should feel so impelled.

Aspiring conductors must surely be expert on at least one instrument, or they cannot hope to establish a working relationship and sympathy with the players. After a few years of preoccupation with technical problems, it should be clear whether the senses of sonority and movement have developed at all. Without these it is useless to aim at the highest opportunities, but young conductors should not be discouraged, if they seem to lack the star quality so eagerly sought in the concert-hall, as there is plenty of rewarding work in the opera houses for an expert and unassuming musician.

Finally I must warn musicians against ballet-conducting, because it demands some qualities quite extra to the normal musical equipment, and unfortunately there are so few posts, where first-class musical facilities are available."

ELLIS B. KOHS

Composer; Chairman of the Department of Music Theory at the School of Music, University of Southern California; Chairman of the Los Angeles Chapter of the International Society for Contemporary Music (ISCM); and correspondent for Musical America (1963).

". . . What is the responsibility of the conductor to the orchestra? This is not a simple question easily answered. One must consider what one means by "responsibility," "conductor" and "orchestra." It is further necessary to distinguish between what the relationship now is, and what it might, or ought to, be.

Reviewing the critical words in reverse order, we may first consider what is meant by the word "orchestra." It is obvious that the term encompasses established professional symphony orchestras, semi-professional and amateur community orchestras, school ensembles of various calibres, and that creature of our electronic age, the "pickup" or occasional studio orchestra. Each of these categories (and there are undoubtedly others) has a different relationship with its conductor. A top-ranking professional orchestra must be treated with respect for the high training and vast experience of its members. The conductor must see to it that the orchestra is functioning on a year-round basis, that its morale is kept high, that the members continue to grow, that its potential as a force in the musical community is not only maintained but re-examined periodically to ensure maximum achievement. Semi-professional, amateur and student orchestras have different functions in the community. As avocational or pre-professional activities, their demands and needs are on a different level, their aspirations and goals are different. A studio orchestra is so ephemeral as to constitute an entity in word only, and not in fact, since there is little if any *esprit de corps* or continuity.

By "conductor" one may mean a regular, full-time leader. Or the term may designate that overly fashionable creature, the "guest" conductor, who increasingly shows less and less responsibility not only to the orchestra he is conducting, but to the community and to the art whose purposes he is supposedly serving. The conductor of the professional organization must have a vast knowledge of repertory, styles, periods and instruments, plus a formidable stick technique capable of adjustment to the demands of any musical composition. He must temper his several responsibilities, those to the orchestra (as outlined above), to his audience, to his managing board (for whom too frequently he must play the piper) and to Music itself. The conductor of the semi-professional and amateur or student orchestra is in addition an educator: he must inform his orchestra with the knowledge and sensitivity which the conductor of a professional orchestra may assume to be present.

"Responsibility" in the present context is difficult to define and to assess. The term "responsible," according to Webster, "applies to one who has been delegated some duty or responsibility by one in authority and who is subject to penalty in case of default." Since the conductor is normally appointed by a lay board and not by the orchestra (except by a few such as the Israel Philharmonic), one might say the conductor has no responsibilities to the orchestra but only to his board. Webster distinguishes the term "answerable" which "implies a legal or moral obligation for which one must answer to someone sitting in judgment." One may note here that the conductor is indeed bound morally to serve the interests of the orchestra, the community, and Music. However, since he is not subject to penalty in case of default, he is in a sense not responsible. The solution, or at least a solution, suggests itself as follows: if the conductor is to be truly responsible to the orchestra, to the community and to his art, he must be appointed by a team of experts who represent the several areas of concern. Until this is achieved we may expect to find a continuation of the present condition, in which we find areas of responsibility ill-defined and the musical public ill-served."

DR. WALTER DUCLOUX

Conductor, Professor of Opera, University of Southern California.

"Today, in the 1960's, it seems to me that the conductor's functions are as vastly overrated as they once were underrated. Simple physical co-ordination and a flair for showmanship can disguise lack of true musical leadership for a long time, especially in an age of guest-conducting limited to sure-fire standard works. First and foremost, a conductor should be a "man of music" with a verifiable craft either as an instrumentalist or a singer.

Compared to the latter, a conductor's responsibility is considerably diminished by the fact that he never conducts a wrong note, but at most a wrong rhythm. His mastery of a score is an unverifiable item when it comes to public and critical appreciation. I suspect that, before long, the era of a conductor which actually started with Wagner will come to an end, perhaps to be followed by an era of the sound-engineer. (According to all reports, the era of recitals is similarly heading for a twilight.) This will, of course, not mean the end of music, but only the passing of a phase which saw the emergence of an important coordinator and catalyzer of collective playing whose functions fell victim to the old adage that "power corrupts and absolute power corrupts absolutely" —the conductor."

MAURICE ABRAVANEL

Conductor, Utah Symphony Orchestra.

"Of course, the conductor's primary function is to bring to life the composer's creation. Roger Sessions wrote very eloquently about that and Claude Debussy, in a little-known letter to the first conductor of Pelleas, Andre Messager, wrote that only the conductor could bring to life what he called the internal rhythm of the music. Words, as he put it, depend on the mouth that utters them and so the eternal duty of the conductor is to be not only a humble servant of the score but, as the case demands, a fighter, a defender, a worshiper, an orator, in short—whatever will best help the score at a given time or place and for a given audience.

One could write books about the subject and I am glad that you are doing it. There is a way of bringing a composer's message across without either being a robot who just plays the notes perfectly or superimposing one's personality upon the personality of the score one performs."

BRONISLAW KAPER

Composer. Academy Award Winner for out-standing film scores, such as Lili, Glass Slipper, and Mutiny on the Bounty.

"A conductor should be able to read the score and have the capacity to remember what he reads in it. Not necessarily a photographic memory for the finest details, but well enough to be constantly aware of the form of the work. He has to have conducting technique, which means that he is able to convey in a mutual language, to his players, his mechanical and dramatic intention. Quite often, conductors overdo the conveying of their emotions, in which case, the members of the orchestra feel left out to a certain degree. They feel that instead of being a live group of performing artists, they are reduced to the status of a dead instrument similar to a violin in the hands of a virtuoso.

I believe it is essential that one study and be able to play the classic repertoire at an early age, so the understanding of the composer's intent becomes second nature. In order to subconsciously sense the relationship of individual and orchestral sections, it is helpful to have the experience of performing as an accompanist as well as a solo artist.

The responsibility of a conductor to a composer consists of trying to interpret the work as close as possible to the composer's intentions and notations. I feel that it is impossible for any composer to notate in a score a fool-proof image of his intention. There will always be a small area left which cannot be expressed in words or signs. Quite often, a conductor can pleasantly surprise a composer by adding, from his own knowledge, to the original conception of the composer."

LYN MURRAY

Composer, Conductor. Choral Director, film music, television, radio.

"In my opinion the primary function and responsibility of the conductor to his orchestra can be summed up in one word, and that word is: interpretation."

WALTER BEELER

Professor, School of Music, Ithaca College, Ithaca, N. Y.

"It would appear that the prime responsibility of the conductor is to reactivate a composition that was created by the composer. We may say that the music is held in a suspended state on the manuscript. In itself it is not living, but the symbols are there with which to vitalize it. These symbols are suggestions for, or reminders of motion. The most important element in a composition is the basic rhythm; it is this that gives meaning to the melody. If a performance does not evoke some form of response in players and audience it has failed completely. The responsibility of the conductor is to induce, through word, expression or gesture, an empathetic reaction from the performers and finally from the audience.

The patterns of the conductor's beats mean little, but the nature of his beats must reflect his inner feeling for the composition. He must look and act like the music.

Obviously each conductor, in reflecting his per-

sonality, will create an individual musical portrait.
If it were not so, the result would be complete
tedium."

RAYMOND F. DVORAK

Director of Bands, University of Wisconsin Bands, Madison, Wisconsin.

"There is no denying the fact that Arturo Toscanini was one of the greatest of all conductors. The mere mention of his name brings to mind many facets of his work which stands as a noble example for others to emulate.

One of the attributes of this man was his humility, to him it was a privilege for a conductor to perform the great works of music. Once, after performing one of Beethoven's Symphonies over the radio, he paused momentarily, then with great reverence said to the men of the orchestra, "Thank God that Beethoven had lived."

Whether it was Beethoven or George Gershwin (Toscanini's was the first of our great orchestras to perform Gershwin's Rhapsody in Blue) it was the composer who "dictated" how a piece of music should be performed."

MARK H. HINDSLEY

Director of Bands, Professor at University of Illinois. Author of several books covering the subject of bands and methods.

"The functions of the conductor are:

1. To set the tempo with motions which clearly indicate the beats of the measure.

2. To indicate the style of articulation.

3. To indicate the proper phrasing in all its aspects.

4. To indicate the tonal volume and maintain dynamic balance.

5. To give proper cues for important entrances.

6. To secure precision of execution and immediate response to all elements of interpretation by use of gesture in performance, supplemented as necessary by verbal explanation and illustration in rehearsal."

Professor L A W R E N C E   R A S M U S S E N

Head of Music Dept., Adelphi College, Garden City, N. Y.

"I believe a conductor is first and foremost a teacher, whose duty and responsibility is to instruct and lead as surely and definitely as any teacher in the classroom. He should be able to enable and encourage the players under him to perform to the best of their ability (and even exceed that!) as individual performers on their instruments and as orchestral players.

What can he do, what can he tell the players to do, which will improve their playing and make for a better orchestra—the best one which can possibly result from their association with it? One hears of certain conductors of the past and present who were great "trainers" of orchestras. Precisely what did they do? What is the best technique for "training an orchestra"? This is the knowledge which, it seems to me, is of the utmost importance for a conductor to have.

Furthermore, I believe that the members of an orchestra have the right to expect something from playing in an orchestra besides monetary rewards.

Many play in an orchestra for no monetary reward. They have a right to expect to play their instruments better individually, and certainly to improve as orchestral players for having played under a particular conductor.

In order to discharge the above responsibilities, it seems to me, the prime need for a conductor is to *know how to rehearse.*"

DAVID RAKSIN

Composer, Conductor. Member of Music Faculty, University of Southern California. President of Composers and Lyricists Guild of America. Composer of works for ballet, symphony and films.

"The conductor must first of all have the knowledge, the intellect and the intuition to comprehend the *intention* of the composer, as well as what has actually been achieved in the work at hand, which is not necessarily the same thing. He should also have the background to provide himself with an appropriate frame of reference for the piece, which might include its relation to the composer's over-all output and to other relevant music, and whatever other information might contribute to his understanding. He must then have the talent, the technique and such attributes of personality as may be necessary to impose his conception of the music's spirit and design upon the performers—to inspire the performance.

The film conductor has the special problem of synchronizing music with action, dialogue or narration, sound effects, in fact, with any specific detail of the film (including cuts, and movements of the camera) which may benefit from interaction with the music. To do this, he should not only be able to sense what is important dramatically, but must also develop or acquire a highly intricate and meticulous technique in addition to that required of the conductor in other fields. This involves some appreciation of other components of the film medium, ability to apply mathematical procedures to synchronization, and at least a musician's understanding of recording and re-recording problems, with special emphasis upon balance among elements of the sound track.

A good film conductor will be able to achieve any required degree of synchronization without distorting the appropriate pace of the music by having to rush when he is late for a cue, or attenuating the beat when he finds he has chosen too fast a tempo and is about to run out of music before arriving at the cue. Finally, it is not enough to hit the cues and to record at a high average of minutes per recording hour. A conductor who asks more of himself than mere technical competence will always try for a real performance as well."

LEONARD FALCONE

Conductor of Bands, Michigan State University,
E. Lansing, Mich.

"The primary functions and responsibility of the conductor are twofold: (1) To interpret the composer's music. (2) To train the orchestra, band or chorus to perform the music in a manner that conforms to the conductor's wishes.

A young musician who aspires to become a conductor does so because he or she feels that conducting will give him pleasure and satisfaction. As the young conductor grows in age and experience the first manifestation of interest in conducting changes to a more definite goal. In time the conductor will have developed a musical concept of his own which he is anxious to demonstrate through musical ensembles. This concept is developed through a wide range of musical training, experience and background. Eventually, the young conductor becomes fully aware that the objectives, aims, purposes, functions and responsibilities of his chosen profession, is to project to the listener, through the medium of the orchestra, band or chorus, his interpretation of the composer's intention. And that the faithful interpretation of the composer's intentions transcends all other considerations. Consequently, the conductor's main function and responsibility is to train the ensemble he is conducting in a manner which reflects accurately his interpretation and music concept, and to make the ensemble perform artistically.

Aside from the technical aspect of conducting, such as baton technique, and the ability to transmit to the performers his musical ideas, the conductor's function is to develop an ensemble whose tone quality, intonation, balance, blend, technique and general accuracy conforms to his highest musical aspirations.

Interpretation and musical style are closely related. They include such factors as tempi, phrasing, the stressing of certain tones, the elongation or diminution of other tones, sonorities, rhythm, accents, proper bowing or articulation, the use of vibrato, other expressive embellishments, and tone quality. These are all part of a whole based on the conductor's musicianship, interpretative ability and general concept.

Obviously, a conductor should have a good understanding of the techniques and characteristic tone quality of the instruments, a thorough training in music theory and composition; must be steeped in music literature, musical traditions, and above all should have a long and close association with the medium he wishes to conduct—the orchestra, band or chorus."

LEHMAN ENGEL

Conductor, Music Director, Broadway Theatre;
Television.

"Especially in the theatre, it is the conductor's responsibility to create, blend, pace, color and guide the entire performance. On the one hand, he must achieve this by inviting the performers—actors and singers on stage as well as orchestra players in the pit—to join with him in creating what has been written and rehearsed; and on the other hand, the conductor must amalgamate into a single unit all of these separate entities. He should energize the whole. He should temper it to fit into its theatre size. He should imbue all of his performers with the desire to play and sing as well as they are able, and above all, he should make them *want* to give. He should be a leading spirit in establishing a dramatic concentration so that his face, his body and the quality of his gestures function within the mood and framework of the scene's expressivity.

While the conductor functions as leader and welder of the many elements, he must never override the composer's intentions, must never "express" anything that is not inherent in the music, lyrics and dramatic scenes themselves, and if he is to succeed in giving complete life to what has been committed to paper, he must personally behave in rehearsal as well as in performances as a *collaborator* of his fellow performers, allowing them to give what they have to give, escorting them, urging them, but never inhibiting anyone. For, without the people who create the actual sounds, the conductor has no existence whatsoever."

HANS SCHWIEGER

Music Director and Conductor, Kansas City Philharmonic Orchestra.

"I regard, as my responsibility, to make musicians see why I ask certain executions of musical phrases. The whole question, of course, concerns style. As an example, I want a musician to know why the pianissimo of the opening of Der Freischutz Overture is different from the pianissimo of the prelude to La Traviata. Here are two different worlds; The German romantic period with its mysterious aspects and expressions in contrast to the bright and translucent world of Italian Opera.

From a practical point of view, I want the musician to know this difference because it will give him a greater enjoyment of music-making rather than a purely functional execution."

DR. HERMAN NEUMAN

American Conductor, Music Director of WNYC, Municipal Broadcasting System of New York City.

"It has been said, that an orchestra is like a woman. To win them you must woo them. Having succeeded in winning them, there is then the possibility of achieving positive results. The goodwill relationship between orchestra and conductor is the foundation for good music making. Since the orchestra players are artists and human beings, they need not be browbeaten to achieve the desired end.

Conducting is more than just stick technique. The mobility of the conductor's face conveys so much of vital importance—emotion, dynamics, etc. This is the metaphysical aspect of the art and it is a very subtle and thrilling thing.

Since a very large portion of audiences listen through their eyes as well as their ears, the conductor's visual technic and style can frequently clarify the audience understanding of the music. One does not have to be a choreographer to achieve this. All things in moderation."

DR. JOHN VINCENT

Composer, Faculty of University of Southern California in Los Angeles.

"To put it most concisely, the primary function of the conductor is to act as the unifying factor in an ensemble performance. This implies a great deal but, again as succinctly as possible, the conductor, bringing to bear all his powers (musicianship, knowledge, imagination and leadership) draws from the players his conception of the composer's meaning as represented by the score and so transmutes to the audience a performance unified in terms of ensemble, form, style and interpretation.

A highly qualified conductor then is all-important in that all the ingredients of the performance are brought into proper perspective through the conception of a single interpreter."

FRANZ WAXMAN

Founder and Music Director of the Los Angeles International Music Festival. Conductor at Hollywood Bowl and major orchestras in the United States and Europe. Composer and Conductor for films.

"The primary function of the Conductor in relation to his orchestra is to extract from the orchestra the most perfect rendition of a given work according to the sound image the conductor has prepared for himself in his intense study and preparation of the work. In order to extract this sound image, he must be capable of recognizing, during the rehearsal, that which deviates from this image.

These deviations may be technical (wrong notes, wrong phrasing or wrong balance of the individual sections) or musical (conception of a musical phrase, etc.). By being able to correct these facets instantaneously, he must then devote his attention and responsibility to imbuing the orchestra as a whole through that sixth sense of almost telepathic communication which very often raises the total effort of the orchestra to an extraordinarily unified expression of their capabilities.

The Conductor is only as human as every member of the orchestra, and the strictest and most honest self-criticism and utter humility in his approach to the music will carry him, in the last analysis, further than any attempt for self glorification. In other words, the most complete preparation in every detail on the part of the Conductor himself is the prime responsibility toward his orchestra."

NEWELL JENKINS

Founder and Conductor of Clarion Concerts.
Music of the Baroque and Pre-classic eras.

"1. For the musician (and by this I mean also the conductor), music must be a composite of five things:

A way of life,
A religion,
A philosophy,
A profession, and
An avocation.

2. The psychological understanding of conductor and player must be based on mutual respect and interest in each other's integrity.

3. The conductor must obtain maximum results with maximum efficiency in minimum time and with a minimum of friction.

4. The conductor's further responsibility is the understanding of the policies of the orchestra which he is directing, and the execution of these policies to the fullest extent of his capabilities."

JOSEPH LEVINE

Conductor of Omaha Symphony, Omaha, Nebraska.

"The subject of responsibility of the conductor to his orchestra suggests that his prime obligation is to the composer. The rudiments of conducting can be learned in hours. The gaining of a total concept of style, structure, sound, interpretive values takes a lifetime. By dint of this authority and with the gentle tools of persuasion at his command, a conductor strives to elicit from his players a unified expression of the composer's intentions. His power to communicate this to the orchestra is the measure of his attainment.

If he allows his men full opportunity to express *themselves* (even though they have voluntarily given up their individual freedoms to his leadership) and, if, in this process, the orchestra members are made to feel that *they* are *equal* partners in the re-creating of this music, a moving and articulate performance will be the inevitable result.

Perhaps in this way, the conductor is really fulfilling his responsibility to the orchestra and to the composer and audience as well."

DR. ERNO DANIEL

Musical Director, Santa Barbara Symphony Orchestra: Conductor, University of California Symphony Orchestra at Santa Barbara.

"Unlike other performing musicians, the orchestra conductor is not in direct contact with his instrument. He reaches to his instrument via musicians of the orchestra. Thus there is a layer of human element between the conductor and the music he makes. To cope with the inherent complexities of this situation, the conductor should possess qualities in addition to those of musicianship and craftsmanship required from every performing musician.

He should be familiar with the multi-voiced and multi-colored world which the orchestra is capable of creating. Only then is he able to visualize the kind of sound-edifice which the realization of a composition calls for.

The conductor is expected to have a suggestive personality which inspires and guides the musician of the orchestra to follow the conductor's way of music making. Yet, a built-in sense for tact and restraint should prevent the conductor from overburdening and overwhelming the musicians.

Above all, the conductor should possess almost a heroic degree of humility in realizing the integrity and importance of the orchestra musician. Only and alone the orchestra musician, this human life-wire, is capable of connecting the conductor with his instrument, the orchestra.

In the process of music making, it is the conductor's objective to give freedom to musician and to music within the aesthetic boundaries of a composition. It is his aim to create a climate where music blossoms freely. In achieving this he sets free his orchestra instead of oppressing it; he collaborates with the musicians instead of coercing them."

HENRI TEMIANKA

Founder and Conductor of the California Chamber Symphony.

"The primary responsibility and function of the conductor toward the orchestra is to create the finest possible instrument with which to carry out the intentions of the composer to the best of his ability."

LIONEL NEWMAN

> *Conductor and General Music Director, 2oth
> Century Fox Films.*

"In my opinion the primary function of a conductor is to balance the orchestra, and know which detail is important and which is not.

Too much detail is as bad as no detail at all.

I also have the feeling that when one mentions by looking at the back of a Conductor that he hasn't "good hands," he is an intellectual snob.

If a man can communicate to the orchestra what he wants to say, he is a good conductor."

IRVIN TALBOT

Music Director and Conductor, Paramount Pictures Corp.

"In conducting for pictures, one of the primary functions of the Conductor is to breathe *with* the music in order to anticipate each preparation, so that the woodwinds and brasses particularly, can take their breath precisely when they need it, not ahead of time, while awaiting the down beat.

For motion picture recording, when one wishes to superimpose instruments over pre-recorded sound tracks, the Conductor should use a firm beat within the dynamic level called for in the score. The technique of recording for films calls for a clear understanding of the time lag of the various instruments and sections, due to the necessary seating arrangements, number of men, microphone placements, etc. The Conductor must adjust his beats so that all sections will be properly coordinated and the synchronization perfect, especially instruments that respond slowly due to tonal characteristics.

The same idea applies to accompaniments, for soloists, either vocal or instrumental, classical or popular."

10 | *What does the orchestra expect from the conductor?*

"Experience is the best teacher." Presumably, this means that only in practice can we learn what is expected of us, and realize the most efficient application of our arts. The conductor, however, finds this axiom a paradox. The moment he begins his professional activities with an orchestra, one of the most important areas of such information is closed to him.

Tradition and protocol inhibit the players from telling him, directly and truthfully, specifically what they expect from the "man" behind the baton. If he does eventually acquire this knowledge, it is only through intuition, guess-work, and after years of painful frustration. It is extremely important for every conductor to be aware of the primary elements the orchestral player expects him to contribute; and a similar awareness on the part of listeners could help them evaluate a conductor in terms of his response to such expectations.

This chapter can prove a valuable guide for both conductor and audience. The contributors quoted have all achieved unusual distinction for their outstanding instrumental accomplishments and musical erudition. Their words reflect the knowledge that can be acquired only through years of experience.

BERNARD H. GARFIELD

Principal bassoonist of the Philadelphia Orchestra: Founder and member of the New York Woodwind Quintet: Member of the Philadelphia Woodwind Quintet: Master's degree from Columbia University in musical composition and Associate diploma from Royal College of Music, London: Soloist with the Philadelphia Orch., Little Orchestra Society of N. Y. and San Francisco Symphony Orchestra.

"The most important function of a conductor (when directing a fine professional orchestra) is to inspire his musicians by providing an outstanding interpretation of the music performed. The next task is to balance the orchestra so that solo lines are clearly heard in a natural unforced tone. Of course a clear beat is a basic tool for every conductor."

GEORGE MORGULIS

Business Manager, Kansas City Philharmonic Orchestra; formerly violist with New York Philharmonic.

"In my opinion, the principal function and responsibility of the conductor to the orchestra is to develop an atmosphere which will evoke from the players their very best artistic response."

JOSEPH SINGER

Solo French horn, New York Philharmonic Symphony. Formerly, Boston Symphony and Detroit Symphony.

FIRST: We look to the conductor to make the music come to life within his concept or understanding of the composer's intent. He is expected to have a thorough knowledge of the orchestra and its problems, including the extreme potentialities as well as limitations of the various instruments. If the conductor exhibits the sum of concept, knowledge and understanding, every worthwhile musician in his orchestra will find himself rising above his average performance level. The manifestation of this phenomenon is the occasional (frequent only in the case of great conductors) inspired performance.

SECOND: As a string player must have a beautiful bow arm, excellent control of intonation and tone colors, as a wind player must have a clean attack and various types of tonguing, as all musicians must have a highly developed sense of rhythm and feeling of ensemble—in brief "total technique"—so should the conductor be equipped for the "act" of conducting. This means that the motion of his "stick" must be easily evident to every player at all times regardless of dynamics, subtleties, or which part of the orchestra he is facing. Also, the need of the players makes it mandatory for a conductor who wishes to have clear results to actually use a baton which is of sufficient length, thickness and contrasting color to its background (his clothing), and to give an accurate indication, to the furthermost member of chorus or orchestra, of the exact moment of impulse for each beat. It should indicate, beyond a doubt, just which beat is being given, to avoid confusion between downbeats and other beats in the measure. Metre (4/4, 3/4, 6/8, etc.) should be evident and clearly defined at all times including changes of metre. Cueing entrances should be handled in an unobtrusive and purely informative manner.

THIRD: During performance and rehearsal, should an accident occur—such as reed squawk, rosin squeek, cracked note, etc.—the conductor should pass it by apparently unnoticed, since in every case this accident is more evident and more embarrassing to the "culprit" than to the conductor. Even a wrong entrance should be handled in the same manner because a glare or an angry grimace serves only to create an epidemic of such happenings in most cases.

FOURTH: In accordance with all of the technical needs listed above, an efficient rehearsal procedure, of which there are many, is another qualification expected from a good conductor. Inadequate preparation at rehearsal obviously will not lead to polished performances. However, if there is truly complete self-confidence on the part of the conductor, superfluous rehearsing can be avoided and more spontaneous and inspired performances will result."

WERNER LYWEN

Concertmaster-Soloist, Washington (D. C.) Symphony: New York City Center Opera: Recitals, Chamber Music.

"Young conductors should realize that the time of the Toscaninis has passed. Not Toscanini's talents, but his way of dealing with the orchestra-men. Dictators are not liked by sensitive artists, and artistic dictators are even worse. As Concertmaster of a few excellent orchestras for twenty years, I have found that the best musical results are achieved by musical genius and personality and not by the power of hiring and firing. Bruno Walter never even raised his voice in a rehearsal, and conducted some of the greatest concerts and operas ever performed. Conductors should realize that some orchestra members might be just as great musicians as they are, even though they play bassoon, horn or violin, and have to follow their intentions."

H A R R Y   S H U L M A N

*Oboist: First oboe of the Pittsburgh Symphony
under Klemperer; NBC Symphony; Recordings
and concert appearances; solo oboist of the
Casals Festival in Puerto Rico since 1957.*

"The basic responsibility of a conductor to an orchestra is to be thoroughly schooled in harmony,
counterpoint, orchestration as well as composition.
He must possess an exceptional ear, sense of
rhythm and a conception of tone color, before he
can command the respect of his players.

The conductor should study his scores thoroughly from both a musical and technical viewpoint in order that he may communicate with a
minimum of "talking." Remembering Toscanini,
all of his "talking" was the very remarkable art of
his baton technique. Everything was so clear in his
own mind before he approached his orchestra,
and he communicated with you even at concerts,
which also lead to his electrifying performances.

Recordings are a fine means of studying scores
and practising the baton technique (in front of a
mirror if necessary), so that your wishes will be
clear to the musicians. For the interpretive art

form, they offer a magnificent opportunity to evaluate this aural work accurately, without the influence and prejudice of the visual histrionics.

The conductor's ability to listen and adjust as a fine chamber music musician, and being able to balance both vertically and horizontally the musical framework, will demonstrate the depth of his knowledge. For in the words of Pablo Casals in the position of conductor, exhorts his orchestra to "avoid monotony" by having a driving intensity and understanding from the first to last note.

When approaching the orchestra, be certain that everyone is ready; or train them to prepare the moment the conductor mounts the podium. Have the preparatory beat of sufficient size and correct time to be seen and understood by everyone within a 180° arc. Recognize that overconducting can be a hindrance too. Take the issue of subdividing in a retard for example, it would be better to discuss it openly and frankly rather than encounter a disaster.

In correcting intonation of a chord, do not say "It is out of tune!" Be specific and identify the possible area of difficulty. If necessary, reconstruct the chord from many different positions; it will be but a moment before the error is identified. A superb ear among conductors is one of the great gifts, and a point from which most members of an orchestra first praise or deprecate a conductor. Granted that this may be unfair, it is real; unless, the conductor selects and surrounds himself with personnel who have these qualities that are expected of them, then this intonation situation is self-correcting.

This leads me to the subject of auditions. Auditions on an individual basis are most inconclusive and inaccurate. The ideal method would be to invite the prospective member into the group and perform from that position. Both tone and pitch will be immediately recognized. The technical emphasis is exaggerated, for the high level of instrumental teaching and learning today preclude this factor.

Finally, the conductor must have a highly innate sense of good taste both in programming and building an orchestra. He should have the ability and courage to select and surround himself with fine instrumentalists and once selected to allow his musicians the freedom of individual expression within the framework of the conductor's general interpretation. Everyone will then be able to experiment and probe the music to the fullest extent. The conductor's personality and ability to relate to his orchestra in this manner, will create the climate in which the musicians will subjugate themselves more readily to the one and only "Maitre."

WILLIAM SCHOEN

Solo Viola, Philadelphia Symphony.

"The conductor of a first-class symphony orchestra must be a superb musician. Not only should he possess great scholarship, but he should have the ability to convey to a body of musicians his ideas and interpretations. Certain outstanding conductors are even able, through the force of their personalities to achieve a truly distinctive, almost personal sound.

I perfer a conductor who expresses his wishes with a minimum of explanations, and who can communicate his intentions with his baton. After all, he should show enough respect for his craft to take the pains to acquire a clear and precise beat. Of great value also is an effective technique of rehearsing, giving corrections where needed, and avoiding the temptation to return to the opening of the composition after each error. This habit only wearies and antagonizes his musicians.

He should respect the members of his orchestra. On the other hand, the orchestra never fails to respect those conductors who are thoroughly prepared, show sincerity, and have an impressive knowledge of their craft unencumbered by pretense. For such conductors they will play in an inspired manner.

And above all, although he may be a colorful conductor, all his skill and knowledge should be used to project the music and not his own personality."

GEORGE GABER

Professor of Music, Chairman, Percussion Dept., School of Music, Indiana University, Bloomington, Indiana.

"The pursuit of excellence in the thorough comprehension of the music to be performed. To use a parallel, he must be to the orchestra what the true artist is to his palette of colors. He must be expert in the knowledge of the capacities and limitations of both player and instrument. He must possess the superior ability of crystallizing the talent and discipline of this democratic force, the orchestra, and generate its energies for the ultimate achievement—fine music making."

JASCHA ZAYDE

Pianist: Conductor: Commentator Radio Station WQXR, New York City Ballet Company, Recording Artist, Chamber Music player.

"The conductor is many things—teacher, leader, the supreme professional among a group of professionals, the funnel through which must pass the most intimate and profound thoughts of the great masters of musical history.

What it takes to be a conductor is the subject for a different kind of analysis; what the responsibility of the conductor is to his orchestra is quite complicated enough for present purposes.

It seems to me that the last statement of the first sentence above is the key one: the conductor is the catalyst through whom 100 musicians first—and then the audience, experience the power and insight of the language of music.

To get theological about it, without endowing the conductor with anything like divine power (God forbid), the conductor is the Moses of the relationship as between God and the people of Israel—God in this case being the composer. The conductor, then, is responsible to his orchestra as

Moses was responsible to the Priests of Israel: he had to comport himself with dignity, assurance, respect and self-control.

The Bible tells us that it was the human frailty of Moses which decided God to deny to Moses the privilege of leading the Hebrews into the Promised Land. There is a lesson here for all conductors. They are only human, after all. As soon as they abrogate unto themselves divine powers, they are finished.

The conductor's responsibility gives him enormous power for good—and he should not forget that in the best sense of the word he is a servant—of the creator (composer), of his fellow musicians (whom he is qualified to serve by his expert knowledge), and of the large public which hears the music he makes.

There is no higher calling a performing musician can fulfill than by serving in this fashion."

RICHARD C. MOORE

First Horn, Metropolitan Opera House Orchestra: Teacher, Brass Coach.

"From the standpoint of a wind player, there are certain specific points considered basic and expected (or hoped for) from the conductor.

First, of course, a clear and positive beat which leaves no possible doubt of the tempi desired. A beat which indicates, beyond any question, whether the metre is in four—two—one—or three, etc., with a down beat that is clear at all times. Then too, the wind player particularly needs the conductor's understanding in the preparation for an entrance attack or change of tempo. The conductor's preparatory motions and the player's breathing must occur together, and if the baton movement is not sufficiently considerate of the time needed for the various types of sound production, the resulting sound will be less than satisfactory.

Another guide the player looks for at the same time, is the phrasing or dynamic level indications as these also affect the player's breathing and preparation. Whether the conductor communicates these details within the beat with his right hand or with the aid of his left hand, the intent must be clear and consistent. In addition, orchestral players look to the conductor for a feeling of confidence in them. A display of contempt or indulgent superiority only destroys the orchestra's morale and does more to impair a performance than lack of ability. A good conductor will, from experience, understand the wind player's difficulties and show consideration by proper rehearsal scheduling, so the players will not be tired unnecessarily.

All of the above contribute to the human element of the conductor and to the proper attitude so important to the player's ability to give his best."

RAY STILL

1st Oboe, Chicago Symphony.

"First of all, what a conductor should be depends on the level of musicianship of the orchestra he is conducting. At the higher levels, he is free to concentrate on his own interpretation of the score— he does not need, so much, to teach notes. He should be a good instrumentalist himself—and have good physical coordination. He should learn the art of *"under-conducting"*—that is the ability to let the musicians under him carry the performance until it doesn't meet his requirements—most conductors are not clever enough to know that 50% of the time they are 'getting in the way.'"

HAROLD FARBERMAN

Former member Boston Symphony Orchestra (tympanist) Conductor, Composer.

"A conductor's function within an orchestral organization is many sided.

For the working musician a conductor must have the following essentials:

    a) a clear (uncluttered) beat.

    b) an excellent sense of rhythm.

    c) a feeling for balance and ensemble.

(While these are the essentials, it is astonishing how many do not have these qualifications.)

Further, a conductor must be firm (which will earn the players' respect), but not dictatorial (which will earn him nothing from the players).

Most important, the conductor's responsibility is toward the music he performs and toward the men who perform for him. The conductor's greatest asset is his orchestra. If he is not all he should be equipment-wise, his men, *if* he has their loyalty, will pull him through the rough spots.

I believe the supreme compliment that can be paid to a conductor with the proper qualifications is to be called a MAN by those who perform for him. No easy task for anyone assuming the responsibilities of conductor."

ALBERT GOLTZER

Oboe, New York Philharmonic Symphony.

"I would like to feel that I am attuned to a feeling of mutual confidence between the conductor and myself.

From the physical aspect, I must feel secure in the knowledge that when I have need of guidance or reassurance from the podium, it will be continuously available. What I look for primarily is a clear and properly placed beat at all times as well as a definitely established rhythmic pulse. This gives me the freedom to phrase without fear that tempo or pulse will be unexpectedly disturbed, getting in the way of good execution which, in turn, makes for a ragged performance, and possible strained relationship."

JOSEPH ADATO

Tympani-Percussion, Cleveland Orchestra.

"I have found that too many conductors forget that they have to be understood by human beings. They get too involved with "looking good" or "fancy conducting." Under such conditions, I have had to bury my head in the music in order to play my part. I knew that looking at the conductor would only cause me to lose my place. Therefore, I would say that one of the conductor's responsibilities to the orchestra is to have a clear, definite beat.

Another fault that I have found in many conductors is turning their backs to much of the orchestra. These conductors only conduct the melody. They will often turn away from a major portion of the orchestra, leaving them to fish for themselves, in order to conduct the small section which at that moment is playing the melody. They forget that symphonic music, unlike dance music, has no beat which is always constant. In symphonic music there are always retards and accel.; if a section of the orchestra cannot "see the stick," they have no way of knowing how fast or slow the tempo is. From this, I should say that another responsibility a conductor has to his men (the orchestra) is to position his hands (or stick) in such a way that it will be seen by the entire orchestra at all times.

A third and very important observation that I have made is the facial expressions made by conductors when a mistake is made. They seem (all too easily) to forget that the orchestra is made up of human beings, not machines. They somehow forget that mistakes or accidents can and will happen. When a musician does make a mistake, these conductors make such expressions of disapproval that it often causes the musician to lose confidence in himself, and thereby lowers his ability to give the best performance possible. I have even seen musicians who have (upon receiving this type of response) stopped playing or become machines by just playing the notes on the page without giving an effort to any kind of musical interpretation.

It would seem very logical to say that an important responsibility of the conductor to the orchestra is for the conductor to remember that his musicians *are* human beings; that these men are not without feelings and emotions. When a musician makes a mistake, he'll know it better than the conductor, so it is therefore totally unnecessary to make any disfavorable remark or facial expression, for it will only cause bad feeling between the conductor and his men.

Of course, correction is always necessary, and it will always be necessary for the conductor to help and explain to the musician what he wants. I am just saying that he will get better results if he goes about correcting the musician as a gentleman and not a dictator."

ROBERT ROHE

1st Bass: Associate Conductor, New Orleans Symphony.

"There are three main categories to view, starting with the conductor as a personality. 1. Understanding the musician: without attempting to probe this too deeply, understanding the player, his motivation, problems, frustrations and his relation to the orchestra is most likely to be appreciated by the conductor who has "played in the ranks." 2. In the area of leadership, one looks for the man who commands thru his knowledge rather than his authority. 3. The conductor who transmits security and confidence will dominate the playing of the orchestra and can then allow the interpretive elements to come thru.

A second category and perhaps the most important would be his musicianship. He would have to show, 1. Understanding of emotional and poetic content of music, a good receptivity to the multitude of subtle qualities that are inherent in music. He would have to, 2. Have the quality to inspire the orchestra, thru, not only his knowledge but his intensity. In the areas of basic musicality, he would have to display, 3. A keen ear, one that can penetrate the maze of sound and dwell on correct harmonies, phrasing, intonation. In a related area, rhythm, he must display, 4. A sensitive use of rhythm as an interpretive medium, he must be acutely aware of the instrument capabilities in deciding on tempi, and as the rhythms grow more complicated, especially in the contemporary works, he must be as solid as the proverbial rock in his delineation.

The third category, that of mechanics or technique, is especially sensitive from the players' viewpoint. The conductor should display, 1. A clear beat at all times, since any doubt as to beat is likely to result in a doubtful quality to the sound. To an appreciable degree. 2. The conductor should convey his wants thru the quality of his beat. 3. The use of cueing, well done, can certainly solidify entrances, for while all musicians perfect their abilities to read and play the parts without rhythmic help from the podium, there are those passages, that, because of rubato, retards, fermatas, these interpretive devices that interrupt the steady, rhythmic flow, create some measure of uncertainty in the player. The bugaboo of a wrong entrance, always in the remote regions of the musician's mind, can be alleviated with the "double check" of a good cue. The knowledge of the score by the conductor is something that has to be well ingrained, for, although rarely would any mention be made of uncertainty during the daily meetings of orchestra and conductor, if some omission is apparent, the conductor knows it, usually the orchestra knows it, and even further, the conductor knows that the orchestra knows it, so intensive preparation has to be regarded as a must.

While my notes above refer to the player-conductor relationship, the conductor's responsibilities for building a good orchestra do not end there. He must be active in the field of personal relationship with the community, seeking to solidify the orchestra's position, enhance its material benefits like concert hall, playing conditions, improvement of salaries, length of season, fringe benefits and the host of minor aids that encourage the good players to remain, and still maintain a staunchness in eliminating the players whose caliber does not match the present standards that he requires. He is indeed and must remain the leader in the major and minor music producing society, and while the era of the Lord-Master relationship is passing, a new era for the conductor is being born, based on communicated knowledge, competence and mutual respect between the conductor and the conducted."

SIDNEY COHEN

Assistant Principal Violist and Personnel Manager, Pittsburgh Symphony Orchestra.

"There is much that can be said about what an orchestral player might expect from a conductor. However, I would like to confine my remarks to the subject of pacing. Assuming that the orchestra is of major status and the conductor is first-class, I believe it is important to plan the efforts at rehearsals in such a way as to gradually work up to what is to be expected at a performance, but to leave a little peak to strive for by the time the concert takes place. Too often the conductor achieves his goals in advance of the concert; thus the performance itself does not measure up because the best has already been given at rehearsal."

SAM GREEN

Tuba: Cincinnati Symphony; Cincinnati Summer Opera; Goldman Band, New York; Teacher at University of Cincinnati and Cincinnati Conservatory of Music.

"Thanks for giving me the opportunity to give a tuba player's viewpoint, since our opinions are so rarely sought.

First, I believe the conductor should be aware of the problems which can develop as a result of poor seating arrangements. For example: the tuba should never be placed close to the tympany. For one thing, it is difficult to maintain good intonation and proper resonance unless the intonation of the tympani is absolutely perfect; and another hazard is the effect of the percussion entering the bell of the tuba and working back into the mouthpiece. There is also a general unhappiness in the back of the orchestra when the tuba is placed with the bell facing the basses.

I, personally, would like the conductors to consider the size of the breath we must take for the various registers and adjust their upbeat accordingly, although a properly prepared beat is the first and most important element of the conductors art as far as any orchestral player is concerned. The beat should be clear and continuous, so those who have long periods of rests to count can feel confident of their entrances should the conductor fail to give a definite cue.

In rehearsal it would be helpful if the conductor always spoke up loudly enough for those in back of the orchestra to hear him clearly the first time he makes his remarks. And, finally, when a conductor stops for a correction, he should tell the player what was wrong and how he should play the passage in question instead of merely asking him to play it again."

ABE TORCHINSKY

Tuba, Philadelphia Symphony Orchestra: Formerly with NBC Symphony, National Symphony, Washington, D. C.: Broadway, Television, Radio.

"A conductor should be, number one, an outstanding musician and a leader of men so that he can mold and then hold his orchestra together as a singularly great musical instrument to make music as he wishes, yet not breaking the spirit of the group. To me a conductor is as necessary to an orchestra as a pilot to a plane—its destiny is in his hands."

WILLIAM SCHNEIDERMAN

Percussion, Pittsburgh Symphony.

"Although I feel that what is expected of me is an opinion relating to the philosophical aspects of a conductor's relation to his orchestra, I cannot separate the "why" of conducting from the "how to," because the needs always seem to specify the demands.

Thus, if a conductor is to be an effective instrument of authority and leadership, he should be as thorough a craftsman as any of his musicians. Once this requirement is met, all that one can ask for is that he be explicit in his communication, and that he be as consistent as is humanly possible."

FERDINAND PRIOR

NBC Symphony, New York Philharmonic, Ass. 1st Oboe Cincinnati Symphony, English Horn Teacher.

"The conductor should:

1. Study and know thoroughly the works he intends to perform.

2. Know *how* he intends to achieve the results he has in mind—or if not—make clear to the orchestra that he is experimenting or trying to get certain results, and not wear them out repeating things that they see no reason for doing.

3. Know conducting techniques.

4. Take reasonable tempos that are feasible for the ability of his men, and yet consistent, *to a degree,* with composer's directions in this respect.

5. Treat the men not only courteously, but with respect—many orchestral players have greater knowledge and experience than a young conductor. Don't play favorites in the orchestra—it causes resentment.

6. Above all—*conduct* and *don't talk*—let your baton or conducting speak for you. An orchestra is not interested in the history of the composition or composer—they are there to *play* music, and in a *minimum* of *time.*"

EDOUARD KESNER

Violin, Graduate of Juilliard School of Music: National Orchestral Assn.: St. Louis Symphony: Chautauqua Symphony: Baltimore Symphony: presently Principal 2nd with Detroit Symphony Orchestra.

"I think a good conductor has to be a fine performer on his instrument (namely, the orchestra) as well as a sensitive sound engineer, in a sense, so that a fine balance of sound, in any hall, can be achieved.

Also, a fine conductor abides by the *composer's writings in their entirety without resorting to changing* dynamics markings, or true values of notes, despite the fact (staccato) marks are present. I believe it is the note firstly, secondly the dynamic and lastly the punctuation.

We have a school of string playing today which I believe is too far "off the string." As a result of this type of playing, there is no true pianissimo, values are distorted and everything is played on the short side, resulting in a very percussive, but poor sound! Concert-masters can be much to blame for this type of playing, since those who play mostly off the string insist that all the strings play as they do. A good conductor would never allow his instrument to suffer such impair. I suppose discipline, in one way or other, is really something that was never known, or players (and conductors) know more than composers like Beethoven, Brahms."

Index of contributors
to chapters 9 and 10

About the author

Charles Blackman—conductor, violinist, lecturer—enjoys the respect of his colleagues for his extensive knowledge and long practical experience in every phase of musical performance.

He was, for fifteen years, conductor and teacher (of orchestral playing and conducting) with the National Orchestral Association. In addition, he served as: conductor with the New York City Ballet Company and the Symphony of the Air—director and narrator of music education programs for children and adults—director of the Warwick Valley Music Festivals, Five Towns Summer Concerts and Light Opera Festivals in the New York City Center and Boston—conductor for Broadway musical productions—music director of the Garden State Philharmonic, and guest conductor with other orchestras.

His intense participation in the orchestral scene, as a conductor and as a player under the baton of many conductors, makes him uniquely qualified to discuss the role of the modern conductor.

BEHIND THE BATON

*A NEW and TOTAL concept of
the entity we see as the "Conductor"*

This book effectively portrays the "Conductor" in dimensions which enable the reader — interested listener as well as professional musician and student — to grasp the full importance of this central figure, what he is, should be, and why. Through frank and searching analyses, it sheds much-needed light on the interweaving functions and responsibilities that operate behind the conductor's public appearance, and discusses commonly held misconceptions and conflicting theories.

Here, too, for the first time, is an opportunity to enjoy and compare incisive statements by forty authoritative personalities whose collective activities encompass every field of musical endeavor. Their candid opinions—written specifically for this book —offer a rich intellectual treat and provide a most fertile area of reference for all who wish to understand the true role of the modern conductor.

WHAT, in fact, IS the function of the conductor, and WHY?

WHAT is the difference between the "Art" of conducting and the "Act" of conducting?

WHY the conductor's authority? What is its source?

WHY his responsibilities? TO whom? FOR whom?

WHAT is his technique? How is it derived?